D064622?

A Guide to
Fervent
Prayer

Arthur W. Pink

A Guide to Fervent Prayer

Edited by Donald White

Baker Books

A Division of Baker Book House Co
Grand Rapids, Michigan 49516

Formerly published under the title, *Effectual Fervent Prayer*

ISBN: 0-8010-7141-0

Second printing, April 1996

Printed in the United States of America

Contents

Publisher's Foreword

In January, 1944, Arthur W. Pink began a series of expositions in his monthly journal *Studies in the Scriptures* entitled "The Prayers of the Apostles." This series was finally concluded in December, 1949, having run six years. Through the good offices of Mr. I. C. Herendeen, Moody Press published in 1967 the larger portion of the series, that was devoted to the prayers of Paul, under the title *Gleanings from Paul: Studies in the Prayers of the Apostle*. Thus, in God's providence, the remainder of this series on the apostolic prayers was left to be published at another time and place.

It is with delight, therefore, that this volume, *Effectual, Fervent Prayer: Studies in Apostolic Prayer and Praise*, is offered to the Christian public, with the hope that it will take its place beside *Gleanings from Paul* as an effective encouragement to faithful worship toward and communion with the Triune God.

A fresh edition of Mr. Pink's Introduction to the whole series has been made for this volume. However, *no* effort has been made to obscure the fact that the chapters of this volume were originally part of a larger series, the majority of which was devoted to Paul's prayers. It is hoped that the preserving of Mr. Pink's Introduction intact will encourage a comprehension of the unity of apostolic practice and will prompt the reader to read both volumes, thereby gaining an appreciation of the integrity and thoroughness of Mr. Pink's treatment of this vital subject.

Introduction

Much has been written on what is usually called "the Lord's Prayer" (which I prefer to term "the Family Prayer") and much upon the high priestly prayer of Christ in John 17, but very little upon the prayers of the apostles. Personally I know of no book devoted to the apostolic prayers, and except for a booklet on the two prayers of Ephesians 1 and 3 have been scarcely any separate exposition of them. It is not easy to explain this omission. One would think that the apostolic prayers are so filled with important doctrine and practical value for believers that they should have attracted the attention of those who write on devotional subjects. While many of us very much deprecate the efforts of those who would have us believe that the prayers of the Old Testament are obsolete and inappropriate for the saints of this Gospel age, it seems to me that even Dispensational teachers should recognize and appreciate the peculiar suitability to Christians of the prayers recorded in the Epistles and the Book of Revelation. With the exception of the prayers of our Redeemer, only in the Apostolic prayers are praises and petitions specifically addressed to "the Father." Of all the prayers of Scripture, only these are offered in the name of the Mediator. Futhermore, in these apostolic prayers alone do we find the full breathings of the Spirit of adoption.

How blessed it is to hear some elderly saint, who has long walked with God and enjoyed intimate communion with Him, pouring out his heart before the Lord in adoration and supplication. But how much more blessed would we have esteemed ourselves had we had the privilege of listening to the Godward praises and appeals of those who had companied with Christ during the days of His tabernacling among men! And if one of the apostles were still here upon earth, what a high privilege we would deem it to hear him engage in prayer! Such a high one, methinks, that most of us would be quite willing to go to considerable inconvenience and to travel a long distance in order to be thus favored. And if our desire were granted, how closely would we listen to his words, how diligently would we seek to treasure them up in our memories. Well, no such inconvenience, no such journey, is required. It has pleased the Holy Spirit to record a number of the apostolic prayers for our instruction and satisfaction. Do we evidence our appreciation of such a boon? Have we ever made a list of them and meditated upon their import?

No Apostolic Prayers in Acts

In my preliminary task of surveying and tabulating the recorded prayers of the apostles, two things impressed me. The first observation came as a complete surprise, while the second was fully expected. That which is apt to strike us as strange—to some of my readers it may be almost startling—is this: the Book of Acts, which supplies most of the information we possess concerning the apostles, has not a single prayer of theirs in its twenty-eight chapters. Yet a little reflection should show us that this omission is in full accord with the special character of the book; for Acts is much more historical than devotional, consisting far more of a chronicle of what the Spirit wrought through the apostles than in them. The public deeds of Christ's ambassadors are there made prominent, rather than their private exercises. They are certainly shown to be men of prayer, as is seen by their own words: "But we will give ourselves continually to prayer, and to the ministry of the word" (Acts 6:4). Again and again we behold them engaged in this holy exercise (Acts 9:40; 10:9; 20:36; 21:5; 28:8), yet we are not told what they said. The closest Luke comes to recording words clearly attributable to apostles is in Acts 8:14,15, but even there he merely gives us the quintessence of that for which Peter and John prayed. I regard the prayer of Acts 1:24 as that of the 120 disciples. The great, effectual prayer recorded in Acts 4:24-30 is not that of Peter and John, but that of the whole company (v. 23) who had assembled to hear their report.

Paul, an Exemplar in Prayer

The second feature that impressed me while contemplating the subject that is about to engage us, was that the great majority of the recorded prayers of the apostles issued from the heart of *Paul*. And this, as we have said, was really to be expected. If one should ask why this is so, several reasons might be given in reply. First, Paul was, preeminently, the apostle to the Gentiles. Peter,

James, and John ministered principally to Jewish believers (Gal. 2:9), who, even in their unconverted days, had been accustomed to bow the knee before the Lord. But the Gentiles had come out of heathenism, and it was fitting that their spiritual father should also be their devotional exemplar. Furthermore, Paul wrote twice as many God-breathed epistles as all the other apostles added together, and he gave expression to eight times as many prayers in his Epistles as the rest did in all of theirs. But chiefly, we call to mind the first thing our Lord said of Paul after his conversion: "for, behold, he *prayeth*" (Acts 9:11, ital. mine). The Lord Christ was, as it were, striking the keynote of Paul's subsequent life, for he was to be eminently distinguished as a man of prayer.

It is not that the other apostles were devoid of this spirit. For God does not employ prayerless ministers, since He has no dumb children. "Cry[ing] day and night unto him" is given by Christ as one of the distinguishing marks of God's elect (Luke 18:7, brackets mine). Yet certain of His servants and some of His saints are permitted to enjoy closer and more constant fellowship with the Lord than others, and such was obviously the case (with the exception of John) with the man who on one occasion was even caught up into Paradise (II Cor. 12:1-5). An extraordinary measure of "the spirit of grace and of supplications" (Zech. 12:10) was vouchsafed him, so that he appears to have been anointed with that spirit of prayer above even his fellow apostles. Such was the fervor of his love for Christ and the members of His mystical Body, such was his intense solicitude for their spiritual wellbeing and growth, that there continually gushed from his soul a flow of prayer to God for them and of thanksgiving on their behalf.

The Wide Spectrum of Prayer

Before proceeding further it should be pointed out that in this series of studies I do not propose to confine myself to the petitionary prayers of the apostles, but rather to take in a wider range. In Scripture *prayer* includes much more than merely making known our requests to God. We need to be reminded of this. Moreover, we believers need to be instructed in all aspects of prayer in an age characterized by superficiality and ignorance of God-revealed religion. A key Scripture that presents to us the privilege of spreading our needs before the Lord emphasizes this very thing: "Be careful for nothing; but in every thing by prayer and supplication *with thanksgiving* let your requests be made known unto God" (Phil. 4:6, ital. mine). Unless we express gratitude for mercies already received and give thanks to our Father for His granting us the continued favor of petitioning Him, how can we expect to obtain His ear and thus to receive answers of peace? Yet prayer, in its highest and fullest sense, rises above thanksgiving for gifts vouchsafed: the heart is drawn out in contemplating the Giver Himself, so that the soul is prostrated before Him in worship and adoration.

Though we ought not to digress from our immediate theme and enter into the subject of prayer in general, yet it should be pointed out that there is still another aspect that ought to take precedence over thanksgiving and petition, namely self-abhorrence and confession of our own unworthiness and sinfulness. The soul must solemnly remind itself of *Who* it is that is to be approached, even the Most High, before whom the very seraphim veil their faces (Isa. 6:2). Though Divine grace has made the Christian a *son*, nevertheless he is still a *creature*, and as such at an infinite and inconceivable distance below the Creator. It is only fitting that he should deeply feel this distance between himself and his Creator and acknowledge it by taking his place in the dust before God. Moreover, we need to remember what we are by nature: not merely creatures, but *sinful* creatures. Thus there needs to be both a sense and an owning of this as we bow before the Holy One. Only in this way can we, with any meaning and reality, plead the mediation and merits of Christ as the ground of our approach.

Thus, broadly speaking, prayer includes confession of sin, petitions for the supply of our needs, and the homage of our hearts to the Giver Himself. Or, we may say that prayer's principal branches are humiliation, supplication, and adoration. Hence we hope to embrace within the scope of this series not only passages like Ephesians 1:16-19 and 3:14-21, but also single verses such as II Corinthians 1:3 and Ephesians 1:3. That the clause "blessed be God" is itself a form of prayer is clear from Psalm 100:4: "Enter into his gates with thanksgiving, and into his courts with praise: be thankful unto him, and bless his name." Other references might be given, but let this suffice. The incense that was offered in the tabernacle and temple consisted of various spices compounded together (Exod. 30:34, 35), and it was the blending of one with another that made the perfume so fragrant and refreshing. The incense was a type of the intercession of our great High Priest (Rev. 8:3, 4) and of the prayers of saints (Mal. 1:11). In like manner there should be a proportioned mingling of humiliation, supplication, and adoration in our approaches to the throne of grace, not one to the exclusion of the others, but a blending of all of them together.

Prayer, a Primary Duty of Ministers

The fact that so many prayers are found in the New Testament Epistles calls attention to an important aspect of ministerial duty. The preacher's obligations are not fully discharged when he leaves the pulpit, for he needs to water the seed which he has sown. For the sake of young preachers, allow me to enlarge a little upon this point. It has already been seen that the apostles devoted themselves "continually to prayer, and to the ministry of the word" (Acts 6:4), and thereby they have left an excellent example to be observed by all who follow them in the sacred vocation. Observe the apostolic order; yet do not merely observe it, but heed and practice it. The most laboriously and carefully-prepared sermon is likely to fall unctionless upon the hearers unless it has been born out of travail of soul before God. Unless the sermon be the product of earnest prayer we must not expect it to awaken the spirit of prayer in those who hear it. As has been pointed out, Paul mingled supplications with his instructions. It is our privilege and duty to retire to the secret place after we leave the pulpit, there begging God to write His Word on the hearts of those who have listened to us, to prevent the enemy from snatching away the seed, and to so bless our efforts that they may bear fruit to His eternal praise.

Luther was wont to say, "There are three things that go to the making of a successful preacher: supplication, meditation, and tribulation." I know not what elaboration the great Reformer made. But I suppose he meant this: that prayer is necessary to bring the preacher into a suitable frame to handle Divine things and to endue him with Divine power; that meditation on the Word is essential in order to supply him with material for his message; and that tribulation is required as ballast for his vessel, for the minister of the Gospel needs trials to keep him humble, just as the Apostle Paul was given a thorn in the flesh that he might not be unduly exalted by the abundance of the revelations granted to him. Prayer is the appointed means for receiving spiritual communications for the instruction of our people. We must be much with God before we can be fitted to go forth and speak in His name. Paul, in concluding his Epistle to the Colossians, informs them of the faithful intercessions of Epaphras, one of their ministers, who was away from home visiting Paul. "Epaphras, who is one of you, a servant of Christ, saluteth you, always labouring fervently for you in prayers, that ye may stand perfect and complete in all the will of God. For I bear him record, that he hath a great zeal for you . . ." (Col. 4:12, 13a). Could such a commendation of *you* be made to your congregation?

Prayer, a Universal Duty Among Believers

But let it not be thought that this marked emphasis of the Epistles indicates a duty for preachers only. Far from it. These Epistles are addressed to God's children at large, and everything in them is both needed for, and suited to, their Christian walk. Believers, too, should pray much not only for themselves but for all their brothers and sisters in Christ. We should pray deliberately according to these apostolic models, petitioning for the particular blessings they specify. I have long been convinced there is no better way—no more practical, valuable, and effective way—of expressing solicitude and affection for our fellow saints than by bearing them up before God by prayer in the arms of our faith and love.

By studying these prayers in the Epistles and pondering them clause by clause, we may learn more clearly what blessings we should desire for ourselves and for others, that is, the spiritual gifts and graces for which we have great need to be solicitous. The fact that these prayers, inspired by the Holy Spirit, have been placed on permanent record in the Sacred Volume declares that the particular favors sought herein are those which *God* has given us warrant to seek and to obtain from Himself (Rom. 8:26, 27; I John 5:14, 15).

Christians Are to Address God as Father

We will conclude these preliminary and general observations by calling attention to a few of the more definite features of the apostolic prayers. Observe then, *to Whom* these prayers are addressed. While there is no wooden uniformity of expression but rather appropriate variety in this matter, yet the most frequent manner in which the Deity is addressed is as Father: "the Father of mercies" (II Cor. 1:3); "the God and Father of our Lord Jesus Christ" (Eph. 1:3; I Peter 1:3); "the Father of glory" (Eph. 1:17); "the Father of our Lord Jesus Christ" (Eph. 3:14). In this language we see clear evidence of how the holy apostles took heed to the injunction of their Master. For when they made request of Him, saying, "Lord, teach us to pray," He responded thus: "When ye pray, say, Our *Father* which art in heaven" (Luke 11:1, 2, ital. mine). This He also taught them by means of example in John 17:1, 5, 11, 21, 24, and 25. Both Christ's instruction and example have been recorded for our learning. We are not unmindful of how many have unlawfully and lightly addressed God as "Father," yet their abuse does not warrant our neglecting to acknowledge this blessed relationship. Nothing is more calculated to warm the heart and give liberty of utterance than a realization that we are approaching our *Father*. If we have received, of a truth, "the Spirit of adoption" (Rom. 8:15), let us not quench Him, but by His promptings cry, "Abba, Father."

The Brevity and Definiteness of Apostolic Praying

Next, we note their brevity. The prayers of the apostles are short ones. Not some, or even most, but all of them are exceedingly brief, most of them encompassed in but one or two verses, and the longest in only seven verses. How this rebukes the lengthy, lifeless and wearisome prayers of many a pulpit. Wordy prayers are usually windy ones. I quote again from Martin Luther, this time from his comments on the Lord's prayer directed to simple laymen:

> When thou prayest let thy words be few, but thy thoughts and affections many, and above all let them be profound. The less thou speakest the better thou prayest. . . . External and bodily prayer is that buzzing of the lips, that outside babble that is gone through without any attention, and which strikes the ears of men; but prayer in spirit and in truth is the inward desire, the motions, the sighs, which issue from the depths of the heart. The former is the prayer of hypocrites and of all who trust in themselves: the latter is the prayer of the children of God, who walk in His fear.

Observe, too, their definiteness. Though exceedingly brief, yet their prayers are very explicit. There were no vague ramblings or mere generalizations, but specific requests for definite things. How much failure there is at this point. How many prayers have we heard that were so incoherent and aimless, so lacking in point and unity, that when the Amen was reached we could scarcely remember one thing for which thanks had been given or request had been made! Only a blurred impression remained on the mind, and a feeling that the supplicant had engaged more in a form of indirect preaching than direct praying. But examine any of the prayers of the apostles and it will be seen at a glance that theirs are like those of their Master's in Matthew 6:9-13 and John 17, made up of definitive adorations and sharply-defined petitions. There is neither moralizing nor uttering of pious platitudes, but a spreading before God of certain needs and a simple asking for the supply of them.

The Burden and Catholicity of the Apostles' Prayers

Consider also the burden of them. In the recorded apostolic prayers there is no supplicating God for the supply of temporal needs and (with a single exception) no asking Him to interpose on their behalf in a providential way (though petitions for these things are legitimate when kept in proper proportion to spiritual concerns. Instead, the things asked for are wholly of a spiritual and gracious nature: that the Father may give unto us the spirit of understanding and revelation in the knowledge of Himself, the eyes of our understanding being enlightened so that we may know what is the hope of His calling, the riches of the glory of His inheritance in the saints, and the exceeding greatness of His power to usward who believe (Eph. 1: 17-19); that He would grant us, according to the riches of His glory, to be strengthened with might by His Spirit in the inner man, that Christ may dwell in our hearts by faith, that we might know the love of Christ which passeth knowledge, and be filled with all the fulness of God (Eph. 3:16-19); that our love may abound more and more, that we might be sincere and without offense, and be filled with the fruits of righteousness (Phil. 1:9-11); that we might walk worthy of the Lord unto all pleasing (Col. 1:10); that we might be sanctified wholly (I Thess. 5:23).

Note also the catholicity of them. Not that it is either wrong or unspiritual to pray for ourselves individually, any more than it is to supplicate for temporal and providential mercies; I mean, rather, to direct attention to where the apostles placed *their* emphasis. In one only do we find Paul praying for himself, and rarely for particular individuals (as is to be expected with prayers that are a part of the public record of Holy Scripture, though no doubt he prayed much for individuals in secret). His general custom was to pray for the whole household of faith. In this he adheres closely to the pattern prayer given us by Christ, which I like to think of as the Family Prayer. All its pronouns are in the plural number: "Our Father," "give us" (not only "me"), "forgive us," and so forth. Accordingly we find the Apostle Paul exhorting us to be making "supplication for *all* saints" (Eph. 6:18, ital. mine), and in his prayers he sets us an example of this very thing. He pleaded with the Father that the Ephesian church might "be able to comprehend with *all* saints what is the breadth, and length, and depth, and height; And to know the love of Christ, which passeth knowledge" (Eph. 3:18, ital. mine). What a corrective for self-centeredness! If I am praying for "all saints," I include myself!

A Striking Omission

Finally, let me point out a striking omission. If all the apostolic prayers be read attentively, it will be found that in none of them is any place given to that which occupies such prominence in the prayers of Arminians. Not once do we find God asked to save the world in general or to pour out His Spirit on all flesh without exception. The apostles did not so much as pray for the conversion of an entire city in which a particular Christian church was located. In this they conformed again to the example set for them by Christ: "I pray not for the world," said He, "but for them which thou hast given me" (John 17:9). Should it be objected that the Lord Jesus was there praying only for His immediate apostles or disciples, the answer is that when He extended His prayer beyond them it was not for the world that He prayed, but only for His believing people until the end of time (see John 17:20, 21). It is true that Paul teaches "that supplications, prayers, intercessions, and giving of thanks, be made for all [classes of] men; for kings, and for all that are in authority" (I Tim. 2:1, 2a, brackets mine)—in which duty many are woefully remiss—yet it is not for their salvation, but "that *we* may lead a quiet and peaceable life in all godliness and honesty" (v. 2b, ital. mine). There is much to be learned from the prayers of the apostles.

1

Hebrews 13:20, 21

Part I

This prayer contains a remarkable epitome of the entire epistle—an epistle to which every minister of the Gospel should devote special attention. Nothing else is so much needed today as expository sermons on the Epistles to the Romans and to the Hebrews: the former supplies that which is best suited to repel the legalism, antinomianism and Arminianism that are now so rife, while the latter refutes the cardinal errors of Rome and exposes the sacerdotal pretensions of her priests. It provides the Divine antidote to the poisonous spirit of ritualism that is now making such fatal inroads into so many sections of a decadent Protestantism. That which occupies the central portion in this vitally important and most blessed treatise is the priesthood of Christ, which embodies the substance of what was foreshadowed both in Melchizedek and Aaron. In the Book of Hebrews it is shown that His one perfect sacrifice has forever displaced the Levitical institutions and made an end of the whole Judaic system. That all-sufficient oblation of the Lord Jesus made complete atonement for the sins of His people, fully satisfying every legal claim that God's Law had upon them, thereby rendering needless any efforts of theirs to placate Him. "For by one offering he hath perfected for ever them that are sanctified" (Heb. 10:14). That is to say, Christ has infallibly, irrevocably set apart to the service of God those who have believed, and that by the excellence of His finished work.

The Resurrection Declares God's Acceptance of Christ's Work

God's acceptance of Christ's atoning sacrifice was demonstrated by His raising Christ from the dead and setting Him at the right hand of the Majesty on high. That which characterized Judaism was sin, death, and distance from God—the perpetual shedding of blood and the people shut out from the Divine presence. But that which marks Christianity is a risen and enthroned Savior, who has put away the sins of His people from before the face of God and has secured for them the right of access to Him. "Having therefore, brethren, boldness [liberty] to enter into the holiest by the blood of Jesus, By a new and living way, which he hath consecrated for us, through the veil, that is to say, his flesh; And having an high priest over the house of God; Let us draw near with a true heart in full assurance of faith" (Heb. 10:19-22a, brackets mine). Thus we are encouraged to draw nigh to God with full confidence in the infinite merits of Christ's blood and righteousness, depending entirely thereon. In his prayer, the apostle makes request that the whole of what he had set before them in the doctrinal part of the Epistle might be effectually applied to their hearts. In a brief but comprehensive sentence, Paul prays that there might be worked out in the lives of the redeemed Hebrews every grace and virtue to which he had exhorted them in the previous chapters. We shall consider the object, plea, request, and doxology of this benedictory invocation.

The Divine Titles Invoked Discriminately

"The God of peace" is the One to whom this prayer is directed. As I intimated in some of the chapters of my book called *Gleanings from Paul*, the various titles by which the apostles addressed the Deity were not used at random, but were chosen with spiritual discrimination. They were neither so poverty-stricken in language as to always supplicate God under the same name, nor were they so careless as to speak with Him under the first one that came to mind. Instead, in their approaches to Him they carefully singled out that attribute of the Divine nature, or that particular relationship that God sustains to His people, which most accorded with the specific blessing they sought. The same principle of discrimination appears in the Old Testament prayers. When holy men of old sought strength, they looked to the Mighty One. When they desired forgiveness, they appealed to "the multitude of his tender mercies." When they cried for deliverance from their enemies, they pleaded His covenant faithfulness.

The God of Peace

I dwelt upon this title "the God of peace" in chapter 4 of *Gleanings from Paul* (pp. 41-46), but would like to explicate it further with several lines of thought.

First, it is a distinctively *Pauline* title, since no other New Testament writer employs the expression. Its usage here is one of the many internal proofs that he was the penman of this Epistle. It occurs six times in his writings:

Romans 15:33, and 16:20; II Corinthians 13:11; Philippians 4:9; I Thessalonians 5:23; and here in Hebrews 13:20; "the Lord of peace" is used once in II Thessalonians 3:16. It is therefore evident that Paul had a special delight in contemplating God in this particular character. And well he might, for it is an exceedingly blessed and comprehensive one; and for that reason I have done my best, according to the measure of light granted to me, to open its meaning. A little later I shall suggest why Paul, rather than any of the other of the apostles, coined this expression.

Secondly, it is a *forensic* title, viewing God in His official character as Judge. It tells us that He is now reconciled to believers. It signifies that the enmity and strife that formerly existed between God and elect sinners is now ended. The previous hostility had been occasioned by man's apostasy from his Maker and Lord. The entrance of sin into this world disrupted the harmony between heaven and earth, severed communion between God and man, and ushered in discord and strife. Sin evoked God's righteous displeasure and called for His judicial action. Mutual alienation ensued; for a holy God cannot be at peace with sin, being "angry with the wicked every day" (Ps. 7:11). But Divine wisdom had devised a way whereby rebels could be restored to His favor without the slightest diminution of His honor. Through the obedience and sufferings of Christ full reparation was made to the Law and peace was reestablished between God and sinners. By the gracious operations of God's Spirit, the enmity that was in the hearts of His people is overcome, and they are brought into loyal subjection to Him. Thereby the discord has been removed and amity created.

Thirdly, it is a *restrictive* title. God is "the God of peace" only to those who are savingly united to Christ, for there is now no condemnation to those who are in Him

(Rom. 8:1). But the case is far different with those who refuse to bow to the scepter of the Lord Jesus and take shelter beneath His atoning blood. "He that believeth on the Son hath everlasting life: and he that believeth not the Son shall not see life; but the wrath of God abideth on him" (John 3:36). Notice that it is not that the sinner shall yet fall beneath God's wrath of the Divine Law, but that he is already under it. "For the wrath of God is revealed from heaven against *all* ungodliness and unrighteousness of men" (Rom. 1:18, ital. mine). Furthermore, by virtue of their federal relationship to Adam, all his descendants are "by nature the children of wrath" (Eph. 2:3), entering this world as the objects of God's judicial displeasure. So far from being "the God of peace" to those who are out of Christ, "The LORD is a man of war" (Exod. 15:3). "He is terrible to the kings of the earth" (Ps. 76:12).

"The God of Peace," a Gospel Title

Fourthly, this title, "the God of peace," is therefore an *evangelical* one. The good news that His servants are commissioned to preach to every creature is designated "the gospel of peace" (Rom. 10:15). Most appropriately is it so named, for it sets forth the glorious Person of the Prince of peace and His all-sufficient work whereby He "made peace through the blood of his cross" (Col. 1:20). It is the business of the evangelist to explain how Christ did so, namely, by His entering into the awful breach that sin had made between God and men, and by having transferred to Himself the iniquities of all who should believe on Him, suffering the full penalty due those iniquities. When the Sinless One was made sin for His people, He came under the curse of the Law and the wrath of God. It is in accordance with His own eternal purpose of grace (Rev. 13:8) that God the Father declares, "Awake, O sword, against my shepherd, and against the man that is my fellow" (Zech. 13:7). Justice having been satisfied, God is now pacified; and all who are justified by faith "have peace with God through our Lord Jesus Christ:" (Rom. 5:1).

Fifthly, it is therefore a *covenant* title, for all that was transacted between God and Christ was according to everlasting stipulation. "And the counsel of peace shall be between them both" (Zech. 6:13). It had been eternally agreed that the good Shepherd should make complete satisfaction for the sins of His flock, reconciling God to them and them to God. That compact between God and the Surety of His elect is expressly denominated a "covenant of peace," and the inviolability of the same appears in that blessed declaration, "For the mountains shall depart, and the hills be removed; but my kindness shall not depart from thee, neither shall the covenant of my peace be removed, saith the LORD that hath mercy on thee" (Isa. 54:10). The shedding of Christ's blood was the sealing or ratifying of that covenant, as Hebrews 13:20 goes on to intimate. In consequence thereof, the face of the Supreme Judge is wreathed in smiles of benignity as He beholds His people in His Anointed One.

Sixthly, this title "the God of peace" is also a *dispensational* one, and as such, it had a special appeal for the one who so frequently employed it. Though a Jew by birth, and a Hebrew of the Hebrews by training, Paul was called of God to "preach among the Gentiles the unsearchable riches of Christ" (Eph. 3:8). This fact may indicate the reason that this appellation, "the God of peace," is peculiar to Paul; for, whereas the other apostles ministered and wrote principally to the Circumcision, Paul was preeminently the apostle to the Uncircumcision. Therefore he, more than any, would render adoration to God on account of the fact that peace was being preached to those who were afar off as well as to those who were nigh (Eph. 2:13-17). A special revelation was made to him concerning Christ: "For he is our peace, who hath made both [believing Jews and Gentiles] one, and hath broken down the middle wall of partition [the ceremonial law, which under Judaism had divided them] between us; . . . for to make in himself of twain one new man, so making peace [between them]; And that he might reconcile both unto God" (Eph. 2:14-16, brackets mine). Thus, on account of his having received this special revelation, there was a particular propriety in the Apostle to the Gentiles addressing God by this title when making supplication for the Hebrews, just as there was when he employed it in prayer for the Gentiles.

Lastly, this is a *relative* title. By this I mean that it is closely related to Christian experience. The saints are not only the subjects of that judicial peace which Christ made with God on their behalf, but they are also the partakers of Divine grace experientially. The measure of God's peace that they enjoy is determined by the extent to which they are obedient to God, for piety and peace are inseparable. The intimate connection there is between the peace of God and the sanctifying of believers appears both in I Thessalonians 5:23, and here in Hebrews 13:20, 21. For in each passage request is made for the promotion of practical holiness, and in each the "God of peace" is supplicated. When holiness reigned over the whole universe, peace prevailed also. There was no war in heaven until one of the chief of the angels became a devil, and fomented a rebellion against the thrice holy God. As sin brings strife and misery, so holiness begets peace of conscience. Holiness is well pleasing to God, and when He is well pleased all is peace. The more this prayer be pondered in detail, and as a whole, the more the appropriateness of its address will appear.

God's Resurrection of Christ Our Plea

"Now the God of peace, that brought again from the dead our Lord Jesus, that great shepherd of the sheep, through the blood of the everlasting covenant" (v. 20). This reference to the deliverance of Christ from the tomb I regard as *the plea* on which the apostle bases the request that follows. Since I consider this to be one of the most important verses in the New Testament, I shall give my best attention to every word in it, the more so since part of its wondrous contents is so little comprehended today. We should observe, first, the character in which the Savior is here viewed; secondly, the act of God in bringing him forth from the dead; thirdly, the connection between that act and His office as "the God of peace"; fourthly, how that the meritorious cause of the same was "the blood of the everlasting covenant; and fifthly, the powerful motive that the meritorious cause provides to encourage the saints to come boldly to the throne of grace where they may obtain mercy and find grace to help in time of need. May the Holy Spirit deign to be our Guide as we prayerfully ponder this portion of the Truth.

That Great Shepherd of the Sheep

This title of Christ's was most pertinent and appropriate in an Epistle to Jewish converts, for the Old Testament had taught them to look for the Messiah in that specific function. Moses and David, eminent types of Him, were shepherds. Concerning the first it is said, "Thou leddest

thy people like a flock by the hand of Moses and Aaron"
(Ps. 77:20). Under the name of the second God promised
the Messiah to Israel: "And I will set up one shepherd
over them, and he shall feed them, even my servant [the
antitypical] David; he shall feed them, and he shall be
their shepherd" (Ezek. 34:23, brackets mine). That Paul
here made reference to that particular prophecy is clear
from what it went on to say: "And I will make with them
a covenant of peace" (v. 25). Here in Hebrews 13:20, the
same three things are brought together: the God of peace,
the great Shepherd, the everlasting covenant, and in a
manner (in perfect accord with the theme of the Epistle)
that refuted the erroneous conception that the Jews had
formed of their Messiah. They imagined that He would
secure for them an external deliverance as Moses had
done and a prosperous national state as David had set up.
They had no idea that He would shed His precious blood
and be brought down into the grave, though they should
have known and understood it in the light of prophetic
revelation.

When Christ appeared in their midst, He definitely presented Himself to the Jews in this character. He not only
declared, "I am the good shepherd:" but added this: "the
good shepherd giveth his life for the sheep" (John 10:11).
John the Baptist, Christ's forerunner, heralded His public
manifestation in this wise: "Behold the Lamb of God,
which taketh away the sin of the world" (John 1:29). In
this dual character, or under this twofold revelation, the
Lord Jesus had been prophesied in Isaiah 53 (as viewed
against the backdrop of Ezek. 34): "All we like sheep have
gone astray; we have turned every one to his own way;
and the LORD hath laid on him [i.e. the Shepherd, whose
the sheep are!] the iniquity of us all" (Isa. 53:6, brackets
mine; cf. Zech. 13:7). Note a wonderful congruity of

expression between the next verse of Isaiah's prophecy (53:7) and the prayer we are studying. Isaiah prophesies, "he is *brought* as a lamb to the slaughter, and as a sheep before her shearers is dumb, so he openeth not his mouth." (ital. mine) Notice how the same Spirit who inspired Isaiah prompts Paul to say in Hebrews 13:20 that God—not "raised," but—" *brought* again from the dead our Lord Jesus, the great shepherd of the sheep" (ital. mine). The fact that God *brought* back again from the dead this great Shepherd signifies that the Father had previously brought Him into death as a Substitute, a propitiatory Lamb, for the sins of His sheep. How minutely accurate is the language of Holy Writ and how perfect the harmony—*verbal* harmony—of the Old and New Testaments!

Peter, in his first Epistle, under the Spirit, appropriated the same wonderful prophecy concerning the Lord Jesus. After referring to Him as the "lamb without blemish and without spot:" by Whom we are redeemed (I Peter 1:18, 19), he goes on to cite some of the predictive expressions of Isaiah 53: that which speaks of us "as sheep going astray"; that which refers to the saving virtue of Christ's expiatory passion—"by whose stripes ye were healed"; and the general teaching of the prophecy, that in bearing our sins in His own body on the tree Christ was transacting heavenly business with the righteous Judge as "the Shepherd and Bishop of your [our] souls" (I Peter 2:24, 25, brackets mine). Thus he was led to expound Isaiah portraying the Savior as a Lamb in death and a Shepherd in resurrection. The excuselessness of the Jews' ignorance of Christ in this particular office appears still further in that, through yet another of their prophets, it had been announced that God would say, "Awake, O sword, against my shepherd, against the man that is my fellow, saith the LORD of hosts: smite the Shepherd . . ." (Zech. 13:7). There

God is viewed in His judicial character as being angry
with the Shepherd for our sakes: since He bore our sins,
justice must take satisfaction from Him. Thus was "the
chastisement of our peace" laid upon Him, and the good
Shepherd gave His life for the sheep as a satisfaction for
the righteous claims of God.

That Great Shepherd

From what has been set forth above, we may the better
perceive why it was that the Apostle Paul designated Him
"*that* great shepherd": the One not only foreshadowed by
Abel, by the patriarchal shepherds; typified by David, but
also portrayed as the Shepherd of Jehovah in the Messianic predictions. We should note that both of His *natures*
were contemplated under this appellation: "my Shepherd, . . . the man that is my fellow, saith the Lord"
(Zech. 13:7). As the profound Goodwin pointed out cen-
turies ago, this title also implies all of Christ's *offices*: His
prophetic office—"He shall feed his flock like a shepherd"
(Isa. 40:11; cf. Ps. 23:1, 2); His priestly office—"the good
shepherd giveth his life for the sheep" (John 10:11); His
royal office—for the same passage that announced that
He should be Shepherd over God's people also denominated Him a "prince" (Ezek. 34:23, 24). Christ Himself
points out the connection between His kingly office and
His being described as a Shepherd: "When the Son of
man shall come in his glory, and all the holy angels with
him, then shall he sit upon the throne of his glory: And
before him shall be gathered all nations; and he shall
separate them one from another, as a shepherd divideth
his sheep from the goats" (Matt. 25:31, 32). He is indeed
that "great Shepherd," all-sufficient for His flock.

A Shepherd Must Have Sheep

"Now the God of peace, that brought again from the dead our Lord Jesus, that great Shepherd of the sheep." See there the relation of the Redeemer to the redeemed. Shepherd and sheep are correlative terms: one cannot properly term any man a *shepherd* if he has no sheep. The idea of Christ as Shepherd necessarily implies that there is a chosen flock. Christ is the Shepherd of the *sheep*, and not of the wolves (Luke 10:3), nor even of the goats (Matt. 25:32, 33), for He has received no charge from God to save them. How the basic truth of particular redemption stares us in the face in innumerable passages throughout the Scriptures! "He did not lay down His life for the whole herd of mankind, but for the flock of the elect which was given to Him by the Father, as He declared in John 10:14-16, 26" (John Owen).

Observe, too, how this title intimates His *Mediatorship*: as the Shepherd He is not the ultimate Lord of the flock, but the Father's Servant who takes charge of and cares for it: "thine they were, and thou gavest them me" (John 17:6). Christ's relation to us is further seen in the phrase *"our* [not *the*] Lord Jesus." He is therefore our Shepherd: *ours* in His pastoral office, which He is still discharging; ours, as brought from the dead, for we rose in Him (Col. 3:1).

The Superiority of Christ the Great Shepherd

The words "that *great* shepherd of the sheep" emphasize Christ's immeasurable superiority over all the typical and ministerial shepherds of Israel, just as the words "a great high priest" (Heb. 4:14) stress His eminency over Aaron and the Levitical priests. In like manner, it denotes

His authority over the pastors He sets over His churches, for He is "the chief Shepherd" (I Peter 5:4) in relation to all undershepherds. He is the Shepherd of souls; and one of them is worth far more than the whole world, which is the value He sets upon them by redeeming them with His own blood. This adjective also looks at the excellence of His flock: He is the great Shepherd over an entire, indivisible flock composed both of Jews and Gentiles. Thus He declared, "And other sheep I have, which are not of this [Jewish] fold: them also I must bring, and they shall hear my voice; and there shall be *one* fold, and one shepherd" (John 10:16, brackets and ital. mine). This "one fold," a single flock, comprehends all the saints both of the Old Testament and the New Testament (see also how the Apostle Paul sets forth this unity of the people of God by his metaphor of the olive tree in Rom. 11). The phrase "that *great* Shepherd" also has respect to His abilities: He has a particular knowledge of each and every one of His sheep (John 10:3); He has the skill to gather, to feed, and to heal them (Ezek. 34:11-16); and He has the power to effectually preserve them. "And I give unto them eternal life; and they shall never perish, neither shall any pluck them out of my hand" (John 10:28). Then how greatly should we trust, love, honor, worship, and obey Him!

2

Hebrews 13:20, 21

Part 2

"Now the God of peace, that brought again from the dead our Lord Jesus, that great shepherd of the sheep, through the blood of the everlasting covenant." We must now carefully consider the particular act of God toward our Savior that the Apostle Paul here uses as his plea for the petition that follows. In the great mystery of redemption, God the Father sustains the office of supreme Judge (Heb. 12:23). He it was who laid upon their Surety the sins of His people. He it was who called for the sword of vengeance to smite the Shepherd (Zech. 13:7). He it was who richly rewarded and highly honored Him (Phil. 2:9). "Therefore let all the house of Israel know assuredly, that *God* hath made that same Jesus, whom ye have crucified, both Lord and Christ" (Acts 2:36; cf. 10:36). So it is in the text now before us: the restoring of Christ from the grave is here viewed not as an act of Divine power but of Divine justice. That God is here seen exercising His judicial authority is clear from the term used. We are ever the losers if, in our carelessness, we fail to note and duly weigh every single variation in the language of Holy Writ. Our text does not say that God "raised," but rather that He "*brought again from the dead our Lord Jesus.*" This sets before us a strikingly different yet most blessed aspect of truth, namely, the legal discharge of the body of our Surety from the prison of death.

Christ's Resurrection, Part of a Legal Process

There was a formal legal process against Christ. Jehovah laid on Him all the iniquities of His elect, and thereby He was rendered guilty in the sight of the Divine Law. Thus He was justly condemned by Divine justice. Accordingly, He was cast into prison. God was wroth with Him as the Sinbearer. It pleased the Lord to bruise Him, to exact full satisfaction from Him. But the debt being paid, the penalty of the Law having been inflicted, justice was satisfied and God was pacified. In consequence, God the Father became "the God of peace" both toward Christ and toward those whom He represented (Eph. 2:15-17). God's anger being assuaged and His Law magnified and made honorable (Isa. 42:21), He then exonerated the Surety, setting Him free and justifying Him (Isa. 50:8; I Tim. 3:16). Thus it was foretold, "He was taken from prison and from judgment: and who shall declare his generation?" (Isa. 53:8). In his most excellent exposition of Isaiah 53—virtually unobtainable today—James Durham (1682) showed conclusively that verse 8 described Christ's exaltation following His humiliation. He demonstrated that the term *generation* there has reference to His duration or continuance (as it does in Josh. 22:27). "As His humiliation was low, so His exaltation was ineffable: it cannot be declared, nor adequately conceived, the continuance of it being for ever."

Condensing it into a few words, Durham gave the following as his analysis of Isaiah 53:8.

> 1. Something is here asserted of Christ: "he was taken (or "lifted up") from prison and from judgment." 2. Something is hinted which cannot be expressed: "Who shall declare his generation [continuance]?" 3. A reason is given in reference to both: "for he was cut off out of the land of the living."

The clause "He was taken from prison and from judgment" does not merely call to mind the fact that Christ was arrested, held in custody, and brought to trial before the Sanhedrin and the civil magistrates. Rather, it primarily reminds us that the straits of humiliation and suffering into which Christ was brought were on account of His arraignment before *God's* tribunal as the Husband and legal Surety of His people (His sheep, John 10:14, 15), the penalty of whose sin debts against God He was lawfully *bound* to pay (since He had *voluntarily* agreed to become their Husband). "For the transgression of my people was he stricken" (Isa. 53:8). The envious Jewish leaders (and their followers), who with wicked hands crucified and slew the Prince of life (Acts 2:23; 3:15) had not the slightest awareness of the great transactions between the Father and the Son now being legally enforced by their instrumentality. They were merely pursuing their rebellion against the Son of David, the popularly acclaimed King of Israel (John 1:49; 12:13), in a way consistent with the preservation of their own selfish interests as men of power, wealth, and prestige among the Jews. Yet in their high treason against the Lord of glory, whom they knew not (I Cor. 2:8) they did God's bidding (Acts 2:23; 4:25-28; cf. Gen. 50:19, 20) in bringing the appointed Substitute to justice as though He were a common criminal.

The word *prison* may be taken more largely for those straits and pressures of spirit that the Lord Jesus endured while suffering the curse of the Law, and *judgment* for the awful sentence inflicted upon Him.

It was to His impending judgment that Christ referred when He said, "I have a baptism to be baptized with; and how am I straitened till it be accomplished!" (Luke 12:50). And it is to the pains and confinement of prison that His agony in the Garden and His cry of anguish on the Cross are to be attributed. Ultimately, the grave became His prison.

The Significance of Christ's Release from Death's Prison

The Hebrew word *laqach* rendered *taken* in the clause "He was *taken* from prison and from judgment" sometimes signifies *to deliver* or *to free*, as a captive is liberated (see Isa. 49:24, 25; cf. Jer. 37:17; 38:14; 39:14). From both prison and judgment the Surety was taken or freed, so that "death hath no more dominion over him" (Rom. 6:9). Christ received the sentence of Divine absolution, just as one who is adjudged as having paid his debt is discharged by the court. Christ not only received absolution but was actually delivered from prison, having paid the utmost farthing demanded of Him. Though He was brought into prison and judgment, when the full demands of justice had been met He could no longer be detained. The Apostle Peter expressed it this way: "Whom God raised up, having *loosed* the pains [or "cords"] of death: because it was not possible that he should be holden of it" (Acts 2:24, ital. and brackets mine). Matthew Henry declares, "He was by an extraordinary order of Heaven taken out of the prison of the grave; an angel was sent on purpose to roll away the stone and set Him at liberty, by which the judgment against Him was reversed, and taken off." In this vein Thomas Manton insists that the clause "who shall declare His generation?" (Isa. 53:8) means who shall "declare the glory of His resurrection, as the previous words do His humiliation, suffering, and death"?

Manton rightly states, "While Christ was in the state of death He was in effect a prisoner, under the arrest of Divine vengeance; but when He rose again then was our Surety let out of prison." In a most helpful way he goes on to show that the peculiar force of the phrase "*brought again from the dead*" is best explained by the dignified carriage of the apostles when they were unlawfully cast into prison. The next day the magistrates sent sergeants to the prison, bidding their keeper to let them go. But Paul refused to be "thrust . . . out privily" and remained there until the magistrates themselves formally "*brought them out*" (Acts 16:35-39, ital. mine). So it was with Christ: He did not break out of prison. As God had "delivered him up" to death (Rom. 8:32), so He "brought [Him] again from the dead." Says Manton,

> It was as it were an acquittal from those debts of ours which He undertook to pay: as Simeon was dismissed when the conditions were performed, and Joseph was satisfied with a sight of his brother, he "brought Simeon out unto them" (Gen. 43:23).

It was God, in His official character as the Judge of all, who righteously freed our Substitute. Though Christ, as our Surety, was *officially* guilty and thus condemned (Isa. 53:4-8), He was *personally* innocent and was thus acquitted by His resurrection (Isa. 53:9-11; Heb. 4:15; 7:26-28; 9:14; I Peter 1:19). By bringing His son forth from the grave God was saying that this Jesus, the true Messiah, did not die for His own sins but for the sins of others.

The God of Peace Brought Christ from the Dead

Let us now briefly observe that it was as the *God of peace* that the Father acted when He "brought again from the dead our Lord Jesus." The perfect obedience and atoning oblation of Christ had met every requirement of the Law, had put away the iniquities of those for whom it was offered, and had placated God and reconciled Him to them. While sin remained there could be no peace; but when sin was blotted out by the blood of the Lamb, God was propitiated. Christ had "made peace through the blood of his cross" (Col. 1:20), but so long as He continued in the grave there was no open proclamation thereof. It was by His bringing of Christ forth from the dead that God made it known to the universe that His sacrifice had been accepted. By the resurrection of His Son did God the Father publicly declare that enmity was at an end and peace established. *There* was the grand evidence and proof that God was pacified toward His people. Christ had made an honorable peace, so that God could be both "just, and the justifier of him which believeth in Jesus" (Rom. 3:26). Take note also of the *relation* Christ sustained when God delivered Him from the dead: it was not as a private person but as the federal Head of His people that the Father dealt with Him, as "that great shepherd of the sheep," so that His people were then legally delivered from the prison of death with Him (Eph. 2:5, 6).

Christ's Petitions for His Own Deliverance

It is very blessed to learn from the Psalms—where much light, not given in the New Testament, is cast upon the heart exercises of the Mediator—that Christ supplicated God for deliverance from the tomb. In Psalm 88 (the prophetic subject matter of which is the passion of the Lord Jesus) we find Him saying, "Let my prayer come before thee: incline thine ear unto my cry; For my soul is full of troubles: and my life draweth nigh unto the grave: (vv. 2, 3). Since the transgressions of His people had been imputed to Him, those "troubles" were the sorrows and anguish that He experienced when the wages that were due to the sins of His people were inflicted and executed upon Him. He went on to exclaim to God, "Thou hast laid me in the lowest pit, in darkness, in the deeps. Thy wrath lieth hard upon me, and thou hast afflicted me with all thy waves" (vv. 6, 7). There we are granted an insight into what the Savior felt in His soul under the stroke of God, as He endured all that was contained in the Father's just and holy curse upon sin. He could not have been brought into a lower state. He was in total darkness, the sun for a season refusing to shine upon Him, as God hid His face from Him. The sufferings of Christ's soul were tantamount to "the second death." He suffered the whole of what was for Him, as the God-man, the equivalent of an eternity in hell.

The smitten Redeemer went on to say, "I am shut up, and I cannot come forth" (v. 8). None but the Judge could lawfully deliver Him. "Wilt thou shew wonders to the dead? shall the dead arise and praise thee?" (v. 10). In his remarkable exposition, S. E. Pierce declared:

> Those questions contain the most powerful plea Christ Himself could urge before the Father for His own emerging out of His present state of suffering and for His resurrection from the power of death. "Shall the dead arise and praise Thee?" Yet in Me Thou *wilt* show wonders in raising My body from the grave, or the salvation of Thine

elect cannot be completed, nor Thy glory in the same fully shine forth. Thy wonders cannot be declared; the elect dead cannot rise again and praise Thee, as they must, but on the footing of My being raised up.

"But unto Thee have I cried, O LORD" (v. 13). What light this Psalm casts upon these words of the apostle concerning Christ: "Who in the days of his flesh, when he had offered up prayers and supplications with strong crying and tears unto him that was able to save him from death, and was heard . . ." (Heb. 5:7). In the prophetic language of Psalm 2:8, God the Father says to His Son, "*Ask* of Me, and I shall give thee the heathen for thine inheritance, and the uttermost parts of the earth for thy possession." (ital. mine) In like manner, our Lord first cried for His deliverance from the prison of the tomb, and then the Father "brought him forth" in answer to His cry. Behold how perfectly the Son of man is conformed to our utter dependence on God. He, too, though the Sinless One, must pray for those blessings that God had already promised Him!

Through the Blood of the Everlasting Covenant

In the last place, consider that the great act of God here spoken of is said to be "through the blood of the everlasting covenant." As to the exact meaning of these words there has been no little confusion in the minds of different writers on this Epistle; and while a full canvassing of this interesting question is really outside the scope of the present article, yet some of the more erudite of our readers would be displeased if we failed to make a few remarks thereon. So I shall ask others kindly to bear with me while I deal with a somewhat technical detail. A careful reading through of the Epistle to the Hebrews shows that mention is made therein of "the covenant" (10:29), "a better covenant" (8:6), "a new covenant" (8:8), and here to "the everlasting covenant." Not a few able men have concluded that reference is made to the same thing throughout, but with them I cannot agree. It is quite clear from Hebrews 8:6-13 that the *new* and *better* covenant made with the *spiritual* Israel and Judah (that is, the Church) stands in opposition to the *first* (v. 7) or *old* (v. 13) covenant made with the nation of Israel at Sinai (that is "Israel after the flesh"). In other words, the contrast is between Judaism and Christianity under two different covenants or economies, whereas "the everlasting covenant" is the antitheses of that covenant of works made with Adam as the federal head of the human race.

Though the covenant of works was first in manifestation, the everlasting covenant, or covenant of grace, was first in origination. In all things Christ must have the preeminence (Col. 1:18), and thus God entered into compact with Him before Adam was created. That compact has been variously designated as the "covenant of redemption" and the "covenant of grace." In it God made full arrangements and provisions for the salvation of His elect. That everlasting covenant has been administered, under different economies, throughout human history, the blessings of the same being bestowed on favored individuals all through the ages. Under the Old Covenant, or Judaism, the requirements and provisions of the everlasting covenant were typified or foreshadowed particularly by means of the moral and ceremonial law; under the New Covenant, or Christianity, its requirements and provisions are set forth and proclaimed in and by the Gospel. In every generation repentance, faith, and obedience have been required of those who would (and do) partake of its inestimable blessings (Isa. 55:3). In his *Outlines of Theology*, the renowned theologian A. A. Hodge says this:

> The phrase "mediator of the covenant" is applied to Christ three times in the New Testament (Heb. 8:6; 9:15; 12:24), but as in each case the term for covenant is qualified by either the adjective "new" or "better," it evidently here is used to designate *not* the covenant of grace properly, but that new *dispensation* of that eternal covenant which Christ introduced in person in contrast with the less perfect administration of it which was instrumentally introduced by Moses.

Christ, the Mediator of an Everlasting Covenant

Thus we take those words "the blood of the everlasting covenant" at their face value, as referring to the eternal compact that God entered into with Christ. In the light of the preceding phrases of Hebrews 13:20, it is evident that "the blood of the everlasting covenant" has a threefold connection. First, it is connected to the Divine title here employed. God became historically "the God of peace" when Christ made propitiation and confirmed the eternal compact with His own blood (Col. 1:20). From before the foundation of the world God had purposed and planned that peace between Himself and sinful men (Luke 2:13, 14) that Christ was to make; everything connected with the same had been eternally agreed upon between Them. Secondly, it points to the fact of Christ's death. As the righteous Judge of all, God the Father was moved by the shedding of Christ's precious blood to restore Him from the grave and to exalt Him to a place of supreme honor and authority (Matt. 28:18; Phil. 2:5-11). Since the Surety had fully carried out His part of the contract, it behooved the Ruler of this world to deliver Him from prison as that which was righteously due to Him. Thirdly, this blessed phrase is connected to Christ's office. It was by the shedding of His blood for them, according to covenant agreement, that our Lord Jesus became "that great shepherd of the sheep," the One who would seek out God's elect, bring them into the fold, and there minister to, provide for, and protect them (John 10:11, 15).

God's bringing back our Lord Jesus from the dead was not done simply by contract, but also on account of His merits, and therefore it is attributed not barely to "the covenant" but to "the blood" of it. As God the Son, He merited or purchased it not, for honor and glory were His due; but as the God-man Mediator He earned His deliverance from the grave as a just reward for His obedience and sufferings. Moreover, it was not as a private person but as the Head of His people that He was delivered, and that ensured their deliverance also. If *He* was restored from the tomb "through the blood of the everlasting covenant," equally so must *they* be. Scripture ascribes our deliverance from the grave not only to the death of Christ but to His resurrection as well. "For if we believe that Jesus died and rose again, even so them also which sleep in Jesus will God bring with him: (I Thess. 4:14; cf. Rom. 4:25). Thus assurance is given to the Church of its full and final redemption. God expressly made promise to the Shepherd of old: "As for thee also, by the blood of thy covenant I have sent forth thy prisoners out of the pit wherein is no water [that is, the grave]" (Zech. 9:11, brackets mine). As it was "by his own blood he entered in once into the holy place" (Heb. 9:12), so also on the ground of the infinite value of that blood we also enter the heavenly throne room (Heb. 10:19). As He declared, "because I live, ye shall live also" (John 14:19).

The Well-grounded Petition

We turn now to the petition itself. "Now the God of peace . . . Make you perfect in every good work to do his will, working in you that which is wellpleasing in his sight, through Jesus Christ." This verse is intimately related to the whole of the preceding one, and the blessed connection between them inculcates a lesson of great practical importance. It may be stated, simply, as follows: God's wondrous working in the past should deepen our confidence in Him and make us to seek at His hands blessings and mercies for the present. Since He so graciously provided such a Shepherd for the sheep, since He has been pacified toward us and not a frown now remains upon His face, since He has so gloriously displayed both His power and His righteousness in bringing back Christ from the dead, a continuance of His favor may be safely counted upon. We should expectantly look to Him day by day for all needed supplies of grace. The One who raised our Savior is well able to quicken us and make us fruitful to every good work. Let us therefore eye "the God of peace" and plead "the blood of the everlasting covenant" in every approach to the mercyseat.

More specifically, God's bringing back Christ from the dead is His infallible guarantee to us that He will fulfill all His promises to the elect, even all the blessings of the everlasting covenant. This is clear from Acts 13:32-34: "And we declare unto you glad tidings, how that the promise which was made unto the fathers, God hath fulfilled the same unto us their children, in that He hath raised up Jesus again . . . and as concerning that He raised Him from the dead . . . He said [by that action], I will give you the sure mercies of David." (brackets mine) By restoring Christ from the dead, God fulfilled the grand promise made to the Old Testament saints (in which all His promises were virtually contained) and gave pledge for the performance and accomplishment of all future ones, thereby giving virtue to them. The "sure mercies of David" are the blessings that God swore to in the everlasting covenant (Isa. 55:3). The shedding of Christ's blood ratified, sealed, and established forever every article in that covenant. By bringing Him back from the dead God has ensured to His people that He will infallibly bestow upon them all those benefits which Christ obtained for them by His sacrifice. All those blessings of regeneration, pardon, cleansing, reconciliation, adoption, sanctification, preservation, and glorification were given to Christ for His redeemed, and are safe in His hand.

By His mediatorial work Christ has opened a way whereby God can bestow, consistently with all the glory of His perfections, all the good things that flow from those Divine perfections. As Christ's death was necessary that believers might receive those "sure mercies" according to the Divine counsels, so His resurrection was equally indispensable, so that living in heaven He might impart them to us as the fruits of His travail and the reward of His victory. God has fulfilled to Christ every article for which He engaged in the everlasting covenant: He has brought Him from the dead, exalted Him to His own right hand, invested Him with honor and glory, seated Him upon the mediatorial throne, and given Him that Name which is above every name. And what God has done for Christ, the Head, is the guarantee that He will perform all that He has promised to Christ's members. It is a most glorious and blessed consideration that our all, both for time and eternity, depends wholly upon what passed between the Father and Jesus Christ: that God the Father remembers and is faithful to His engagements to the Son, and that we are in His hand (John 10:27-30). When faith truly apprehends that grand fact, all fear and uncertainty is at an end; all legality and talking about our unworthiness silenced. "Worthy is the Lamb" becomes our theme and song!

This Kind of Praying Produces Spiritual Stability

How tranquilizing and stabilizing it is to us when we consider that *we* have a personal interest in all the eternal acts that passed between God the Father and the Lord Christ on our behalf even before man was created, as well as in all those acts that were transacted between the Father and the Son in and throughout the whole of His mediatorial work that He wrought and finished here below. It is this covenant salvation, in its full blessedness and efficacy, apprehended by faith, that alone can lift us out of ourselves and above our spiritual enemies, that can enable us to triumph over our present corruptions, sins, and miseries. It is wholly a subject for *faith* to be engaged with, for feelings can never provide the basis for spiritual stability and peace. Such can only be obtained by a consistent feeding upon *objective* truth, the Divine counsels of wisdom and grace made known in the Scriptures. As faith is exercised thereon, as the record of the eternal engagements of the Father and Son are received into the spiritual mind, peace and joy will be our experience. And the more faith feeds upon objective truth, the more are we strengthened *subjectively*, that is, emotionally. Faith regards every past fulfillment of God's promises as a certain evidence of His fulfilling all the rest of His promises to us, in His own good time and way. Especially will faith regard God's fulfillment of His promise to bring back our Lord Jesus from the grave in this light. Has the Shepherd

Himself been raised from the dead by the glory of the Father? Just as surely, then, will all His sheep be delivered from death in sin, quickened to newness of life, sanctified by the Spirit, received into Paradise when their warfare is ended, and raised bodily to immortality at the last day.

3

Hebrews 13:20, 21

Part 3

"Now the God of peace . . . make you perfect in every good work to do his will, working in you that which is wellpleasing in his sight, through Jesus Christ." As previously intimated, there is a very close connection between this verse and the preceding one. Here we have the *request* that the apostle offered up on behalf of the Hebrew saints, whereas the contents of the previous verse are to be regarded as the *plea* upon which he based his request. Just how appropriate, powerful, and moving that plea was, will readily be seen. The appeal is made to "the God of peace." As the One reconciled to His people He is besought to grant this blessing (cf. Rom 5:10). Moreover, since God had brought again our Lord Jesus from the dead, that was a most proper ground upon which He should quicken His spiritually dead elect by regeneration, recover them when they wander, and complete His work of grace in them. It was in the capacity of "that great Shepherd of the sheep" that Our Lord Jesus was raised by His gracious Father from the prison of the grave, in

order that He might be able, as One alive forevermore, to
care for the flock. Our great Shepherd is presently sup-
plying every need of each of His sheep by His intercession
on our behalf (Rom. 8:34; Heb. 7:25). By this efficacious
means He is now dispensing gifts to men, especially those
gifts that promote the salvation of sinners such as we are
(Eph. 4:8ff). Furthermore, the same everlasting covenant
that promised the resurrection of Christ also guaranteed
the glorification of His people. Thus the apostle calls upon
God the Father to perfect them according to that
engagement.

A Prayer for Holiness and Fruitfulness

"The God of peace . . . make you perfect in every good
work to do his will." Substantially, this request is for the
practical sanctification and fructification of God's people.
While the everlasting covenant has been suitably denominated "the covenant of redemption," we must carefully
bear in mind that it was designed to secure the holiness
of its beneficiaries. We do well to reflect upon the prophetic, Spirit-filled cry of Zecharias, that "the Lord God
of Israel . . . [should] remember his holy covenant; . . .
That he would grant unto us, that we being delivered out
of the hand of our [spiritual] enemies might serve him
without [servile] fear, In holiness and righteousness before
him, all the days of our life" (Luke 1:68, 72, 74, 75, brackets mine). And while it has also been appropriately designated "the covenant of grace," yet we must also
remember that the Apostle Paul said, "For the grace of
God that bringeth salvation hath appeared to all men
[Gentiles as well as Jews], Teaching us that, denying un-

godliness and worldly lusts, we should live soberly, righteously, and godly, in this present world; looking for that blessed hope . . ." (Titus 2:11-13, brackets mine). The grand purpose of the everlasting covenant, as of all the Divine works, was the glory of God and the good of His people. It was designed not only as a display of the Divine munificence, but also for securing and promoting the claims of Divine holiness. God did not enter into that compact with Christ in order to set aside human accountability, nor did the Son fulfill its terms so as to render unnecessary for His redeemed a life of obedience.

Christ agreed not only to propitiate God, but to regenerate His elect. Christ undertook not only to meet all the requirements of the Law in their stead, but also to write it on their hearts and to enthrone it in their affections. Christ engaged not only to take away sin from before God, but to make it hateful and heinous to His saints. Before the world began, Christ undertook not only to satisfy the claims of Divine justice, but to sanctify His seed by sending forth His Spirit into their souls to conform them to His image and to incline them to follow the example that He would leave them. It has been far too little insisted on, in recent times, by those who have written or preached upon the Covenant of Grace, that Christ engaged not only for the debt of His people, but for their *duty*, too: that He should make a purchase of grace for them, including a full provision to give them a new heart and a new spirit, to bring them to know the Lord, to put His fear into their hearts, and to make them obedient to His will. He also engaged for their *safety*: that if they should forsake His Law and walk not in His judgments, He would visit their transgressions with the rod (Ps. 89:30-36); that if they should backslide and stray from Him, He would assuredly recover them.

Paul Turns Messianic Prophecy into Prayer

"Make you perfect . . . to do his will." It was with the contents of the Covenant in his eye that the apostle offered up this petition. In the preceding chapters it has been shown that Old Testament prophecy presented the promised Messiah as the Surety of a covenant of peace and as the "Shepherd" of His people. It now remains to be demonstrated that He was therein portrayed as a Shepherd who would perfect His sheep in holiness and good works. "And David my servant shall be king over them; and they all shall have one shepherd" (Ezek. 37:24). Here the LORD declares that Messiah, the great Seed of David, shall in days to come unify the Israel of God as their King and shall shepherd them all without rival. In the same verse He further declares, "they shall also walk in my judgments, and observe my statutes, and do them." Thus, having owned God as "the God of peace," who has delivered our Lord Jesus from death's dominion "through the blood of the everlasting covenant," Paul makes request that He work in His sheep "that which is wellpleasing in his sight, through Jesus Christ." For though God has promised to do this, He declares, "I will yet for this be enquired of by the house of Israel" (Ezek. 36:37). It is ever the bounden duty of God's covenant people to pray for the fulfillment of His promises (witness the various petitions of the Lord's Prayer). We see, then, that this Spirit-indited, comprehensive prayer is not only an epitome of the contents of this entire Epistle, but also a summary of the Messianic prophecies.

Faith in a Reconciled God Produces Desires for His Glory

"Make you perfect in every good work to do His will." Such a petition as this can be rightly offered only as one contemplates God as "the God of peace." Faith must first regard Him as reconciled to us before there will be any true desire to glorify Him. While there be any sensible horror at the thought of God, any servile fear produced at the mention of His name, we cannot serve Him nor do that which is wellpleasing in His sight. "Without faith it is impossible to please him" (Heb. 11:6), and faith is quite opposite to horror. We must first be assured that God is no longer an Enemy but our Friend, before love's gratitude will move us to run in the way of His commandments. That assurance can only come to us by realizing that Christ has put away our sins and satisfied every legal claim of God against us. "Therefore being justified by faith, we have peace with God through our Lord Jesus Christ" (Rom. 5:1). Christ has made a perfect and eternal peace "through the blood of his cross" (Col. 1:20), in consequence of which God has made with those who surrender to Christ's yoke and trust in His sacrifice "an everlasting covenant, ordered in all things, and sure" (II Sam. 23:5). This must be apprehended by faith before there will be a confident seeking from Him of the grace necessary thereto.

From yet another angle we may perceive the appropriateness of this request being addressed to "the God of peace," that He would now perfect us in every good work to do His will. For the doing of God's will is most essential for *our enjoyment* of His peace in a practical way. "Great peace have they which love thy law" (Ps. 119:165), for Wisdom's "ways are ways of pleasantness, and all her paths are peace" (Prov. 3:17). Therefore it is utterly vain to expect tranquility of heart if we forsake Wisdom's paths for those of self-pleasing. Certainly there can be no peace of conscience while any known sin is entertained by us. The road to peace is the way of holiness. "And as many as walk according to this rule, peace be on them ..." (Gal. 6:16). Unless we genuinely resolve and strive to do those things that are pleasing in God's sight, there will be a state of turmoil and unrest within us instead of peace. There is a deeper spiritual significance than is usually perceived in that title "the Prince of *peace*," which pertains to the incarnate Son. He could say, "I do always those things that please him" (John 8:29), and therefore an unruffled calm was His portion. What emphasis was there in those words, "Peace I leave with you, *my peace* I give unto you" (John 14:27, ital. mine)!

Paul Prays for the Strengthening of the Saints in Their Duties

"Make you perfect in every good work to do his will." This petition sets before us, by clear implication, the human side of things. Those things for which the Apostle Paul made request on behalf of the saints were concerned with those duties that *they* were obligated to perform, but for the performing of which Divine assistance is imperative. The everlasting covenant anticipated the entrance of sin, and it thus made provision not only for the putting away of it but also for the bringing in of everlasting righteousness. That righteousness is the perfect obedience of Christ by which the Divine Law was honored and magnified. That perfect righteousness of Christ is imputed to all who believe, but none savingly *believe* in Him until His Spirit has implanted a principle of righteousness in their souls (Eph. 4:24). And that new nature or principle of righteousness evidences itself by the performing of good works (Eph. 2:10). We have no right to speak of the Lord Jesus as "The Lord *our* righteousness" unless we are personal doers of righteousness (I John 2:29). The everlasting covenant by no means sets aside the necessity of obedience on the part of those who partake of its benefits, but supplies the most affecting and powerful motives to move us thereto! Saving faith works by love (Gal. 5:6), and aims at pleasing its Object.

The more our prayers are regulated by the teaching of Holy Writ the more they will be marked by these two qualities: the Divine precepts will be turned into petitions; and the Divine character and promises will be used as our arguments. When the Psalmist, in the course of his meditations upon God's Law, declared, "Thou hast commanded us to keep thy precepts diligently," he was at once conscious of his failure and said, "O that my ways were directed to keep thy statutes!" (Ps. 119:4, 5). But He did more than just lament the hindrances of indwelling sin; he cried, "Teach me, O LORD, the way of thy statutes; . . . Make me to go in the path of thy commandments; for therein do I delight" (Ps. 119:33, 35). So also, when seeking the establishment of his house before the Lord, David pleaded the Divine promise: "And now, O LORD God, the word that thou hast spoken concerning thy servant, and concerning his house, establish it for ever, and *do as thou hast said*" (II Sam. 7:25, ital. mine; see also I Kings 8:25, 26; II Chron. 6:17). As we become more familiar with God's Word and discover the details of the exalted standard of conduct there set before us, we should be more definite and diligent in seeking grace to perform our several duties; and as we become better acquainted with "the Father of mercies" (II Cor. 1:3) and His "exceeding great and precious promises" (II Peter 1:4), we shall count more confidently upon Him for those supplies.

A Prayer for Restoration to Spiritual Vigor

"Make you perfect in every good work." The original Greek word here rendered *make perfect* is *katartizō*, which James Strong defines as *to complete thoroughly*, that is, *to repair* (literally or figuratively), *to adjust* (see no. 2675 in the Greek Dictionary of *Strong's Exhaustive Concordance*). Contrast this with the word *teleioō* used in Hebrews 2:10; 10:1, 14; 11:40, which according to Strong means *to complete*, (literally) *to accomplish*, or (figuratively) *to consummate* in character (see no. 5048 in Strong's Greek Dictionary).[1] The word in our text, *katartizō*, is used to describe the activity engaged in by James and John, the sons of Zebedee, when Christ called them: they were "*mending* their nets" (Matt. 4:21, ital. mine). In Galatians 6:1, the Apostle Paul employs this word by way of exhortation: "Brethren, if a man be overtaken in a fault, ye which are spiritual, *restore* such an one in the spirit of meekness; . . ." (ital. mine) It was, therefore, most appropriate that this term be applied to the case of the Hebrew Christians, who after believing the Gospel had met with such bitter and protracted opposition from the Jews at large that they had wavered and were in real need of being warned against apostasy (Heb. 4:1; 6:11, 12; 10:23, etc.). As stated at the beginning of our exposition, this prayer gathers up not only the whole of the doctrinal instruction but also the exhortations of the previous chapters. The Hebrews had faltered and failed (Heb. 12:12),

---

1. For futher clarification, both of these words should be studied in the Baker Book House editions of *Thayer's Greek-English Lexicon* and *The Englishman's Greek Concordance*, both of which are numerically coded to *Strong's Exhaustive Concordance*.

and the apostle here prays for their restoration. The lexicons (such as Liddell and Scott, p. 910) tell us that *katartizō*, here translated *make perfect*, literally has reference to the resetting of a dislocated bone. And is it not often so with the Christian? A sad fall breaks his communion with God, and none but the hand of the Divine Physician can repair the damage wrought. Thus this prayer is suited to all of us: that God would rectify every faculty of our beings to do His will and right us for His service each time we need it.

Mark how comprehensive this prayer is: "Make you perfect in *every* good work." It includes, as Gouge pointed out, "all the fruits of holiness Godwards and of righteousness manwards." No reservation is allowed us by the extensive rule that God has set before us: we are required to love Him with our whole being, to be sanctified in our whole spirit and soul and body, and to grow up into Christ in all things (Deut. 6:5; Luke 10:27; Eph. 4:15; I Thess. 5:23). Nothing less than perfection in "every good work" is the standard at which we must aim. Absolute perfection is not attainable in this life, but the perfection of sincerity *is* demanded of us—honest endeavor, genuine effort to please God. The mortification of our lusts, submission to God under trials, and the performance of impartial and universal obedience are ever our bounden duty. Of ourselves we are quite incapable of discharging our duties, and therefore we must pray continually for supplies of grace to enable us to perform them. Not only are we dependent upon God for the beginning of every good work, but also for the continuance and progress of the same. Let us emulate Paul, who said, "Not as though I had already attained, either were already perfect; . . . Brethren, I count not myself to have apprehended: but this one thing I do, forgetting those things which are behind, and reaching forth unto those things which are before, I press toward the mark for the prize of the high calling of God in Christ Jesus" (Phil. 3:12-14).

Divinely Revealed Knowledge Requires Obedience

"Make you perfect in every good work to do his will." May He who has already fully acquainted you with His mind now effectually incline you to the performing of it, even a continuance of solicitous attention to your duties as redeemed people to the end. It is not enough that we *know* His will; we must *do* it (Luke 6:46; John 13:17), and the more we do it, the better we shall understand it (John 7:17) and prove the excellency of the same (Rom. 12:2). That will of God that we are to exercise ourselves to perform is not God's *secret* will but His *revealed* or perceptive will, namely, those laws and statutes to which God requires our full obedience (Deut. 29:29). God's revealed will is to be the sole rule of our actions. There are many things done by professing Christians that, though admired by them and applauded by their fellows, are nothing but "will worship" and a following of the "commandments and doctrines of men" (Col. 2:20-23). The Jews added their own traditions to the Divine Law, instituting fasts and feasts of their own invention. The deluded Papists, with their bodily austerities, idolatrous devotions, and impoverishing payments, are guilty of the same thing. Nor are some Protestants, with their self-devised deprivations and superstitious exercises, clear of this Romish evil.

"Working in you that which is wellpleasing in his sight." These words confirm what was just said above: only that is acceptable to God which conforms to the rule He has given us. The words "in his sight" show that our every action comes under His immediate notice and is weighed by Him. By comparing other Scriptures, we find that only those works are wellpleasing to Him that He has enjoined us to perform and that are performed in His fear (Heb. 12:28). He will accept only those that proceed from love (II Cor. 5:14), and that are done with an eye singly set upon glorifying Him (I Cor. 10:31). Our constant aim and diligent endeavor must be nothing short of this: "That ye [we] might walk worthy of the Lord unto *all* pleasing, being fruitful in every good work . . ." (Col. 1:10, brackets and ital. mine). Nevertheless, we must receive Divine enablement in order to do this. What a blow to self-sufficiency and self-glory is this little phrase, "working in you"! Even after regeneration we are wholly dependent upon God. Notwithstanding the life, light, and liberty we have received from Him, we have no strength of our own to do what He requires. Each has to acknowledge, "for to will is present with me; but how to perform that which is good I find not" (Rom. 7:18).

Herein Lies a Pride-withering Truth

Herein, indeed, is a humbling truth, yet a fact it is that Christians are, in themselves, incapable of discharging their duty. Though the love of God has been shed abroad in their hearts and a principle of holiness (or new nature) communicated to them, yet they are unable to perform the good they ardently desire to do. Not only are they still very ignorant of many of the requirements of God's revealed will, but indwelling sin ever opposes and seeks to incline their hearts in a contrary direction. Thus it is imperative that they daily seek from God fresh supplies of grace. Though assured that God shall surely complete His good work in us (Phil. 1:6), that does not render needless our crying to Him "that performeth all things for me [us]" (Ps. 57:2, brackets mine). Nor does the privilege of prayer release us from the obligation of obedience. Rather, in prayer we are to beg Him to quicken us to the performance of those duties He requires. The blessing of access to God is not designed to discharge us from the regular and diligent use of all the means God has appointed for our practical sanctification, but is meant to provide for our seeking of the Divine blessing on our use of all the means of grace. Our duty is this: to ask God to work in us "both to will and to do of his good pleasure" (Phil. 2:13); to avoid quenching His Spirit by slothfulness and disobedience, especially after we have prayed for His sweet influences (I Thess. 5:19); and to use the grace He has already given us.

"Working in you that which is wellpleasing . . . through Jesus Christ." There is a double reference here: (1) to God's working in us; and (2) to His acceptance of our works. It is by virtue of the Savior's mediation that God works; there is no communication of grace to us from the God of peace but by and through our Redeemer. All that God does for us is for Christ's sake. Every gracious operation of the Holy Spirit in us is the fruit of Christ's meritorious work, for He has procured the Spirit for us (Eph. 1:13, 14; Titus 3:5, 6) and presently is sending the Spirit to us (John 15:26). Every spiritual blessing bestowed upon us is in consequence of Christ's intercession for us. Christ is not only our life (Col. 3:4) and our righteousness (Jer. 23:6), but also our strength (Isa. 45:24). "And of his fulness have all we received, and grace for grace" (John 1:16). The members of His mystical Body are completely dependent upon their Head (Eph. 4:15, 16). Our bearing fruit comes by means of having fellowship with Christ, by our abiding in Him (John 15:5). It is most important that we have a clear apprehension upon this truth, if the Lord Jesus is to have that place in our thoughts and affections which is His due. The wisdom of God has so contrived things that each Person of the Godhead is exalted in the esteem of His people: the Father as the Fountain of grace, the Son in His mediatorial office as the Channel through which all grace flows to us, and the Holy Spirit as the actual Bestower of it.

Christ's Infinite Merits, the Basis of God's Acceptance of Our Works and Prayers

But these words "through Jesus Christ" have also a more immediate connection with the phrase "that which is wellpleasing in His sight." Even though our works are good and are wrought in us by God, they are yet imperfect since they are marred by the instruments by which they are done—just as the purest light is dimmed by the cloudy or dusty lamp shade through which it shines. Yet though our works be defective, they are acceptable to God when done in the name of His Son. Our best performances are faulty and fall short of the excellence that the requirements of God's holiness demand, but their defects are covered by the merits of Christ. Our prayers, too, are acceptable to God only because our great High Priest adds to them "much incense" and then offers them on the golden altar before the throne (Rev. 8:3). Our spiritual sacrifices are "acceptable to God by Jesus Christ" (I Peter 2:5). God can be "glorified through Jesus Christ" alone (I Peter 4:11). We owe, then, to the Mediator not only the pardon of our sins and the sanctification of our persons, but also God's acceptance of our imperfect worship and service. As Spurgeon aptly said in his comments on this phrase, "What nothings and nobodies we are! Our goodness is none of ours."

A Doxology

"To whom be glory for ever and ever. Amen." The glory of God was what the apostle eyed. And how are we to glorify Him? We are to glorify Him by an obedient walk, by doing His will, by performing those things that are wellpleasing in His sight, and by adoring Him. The construction of the whole sentence permits us to regard this ascription of praise as being offered to *either* the "God of peace," to whom the prayer is addressed, or to "that great shepherd of the sheep," who is the nearest antecedent to the pronoun. Since the grammar allows for it and the Analogy of Faith instructs us to include both Father and Son in our worship, then let glory be ascribed to both. Let God be praised because He is now "the God of peace," because He brought again from the dead our Lord Jesus, because He is faithful to His engagements in the everlasting covenant, because all supplies of grace are from Him, and because He accepts our poor obedience "through Jesus Christ." Equally let us adore the Mediator: because He is "our Lord Jesus," who loved us and gave Himself for us; because He is "that great shepherd of the sheep"— caring for and ministering to His flock; because He ratified the covenant with His precious blood; and because it is by His merits and intercession that our persons and services are rendered "wellpleasing" to the Most High. "Amen." So be it! Let the praises of a redeeming and propitious God ring throughout eternity!

4

I Peter 1:3-5

Part I

Certain extremists among the Dispensationalists assert and insist that the last seven epistles of the New Testament (Hebrews through Jude) pertain not to all those who are members of the mystical body of Christ, but are entirely *Jewish*, penned by the apostles to the Circumcision and meant for them only. Such a wild and wicked assertion is an arbitrary invention of their own, for there is not a word in the Scriptures that substantiates their claim. On the contrary, there is much in those very Epistles that clearly repudiates such a view. One might as well affirm that the Epistles of Paul are "not for us" (twentieth-century saints) because they are addressed to companies of believers at Rome, Corinth, Galatia, and so forth. The precise identity of the professing Christians to whom the Epistle to the *Hebrews* was originally addressed cannot be discovered. It is vital to recognize, however, that the Epistle *is* addressed to those who are "partakers of the *heavenly* calling" (Heb. 3:1, ital. mine), something that in no wise pertained to the Jewish nation as a whole. Though the Epistle of James was written to "the twelve tribes which are scattered abroad," yet it was addressed to those members of them who were begotten of God (James 1:18). The Epistles of John are manifestly the letters of a father in Christ to his dear children (I John 2:12; 5:21)—and as such convey the solicitous care of the heavenly Father for His own—to those who had Jesus Christ for their Advocate (I John 2:1). Jude's Epistle is also a general one, directed to "them that are sanctified by God the Father, and preserved in Jesus Christ" (v. 1).

Those for Whom Peter Offers this Doxology

The first Epistle of Peter is addressed to "the strangers scattered throughout Pontus, Galatia, Cappadocia, Asia, and Bithynia" (I Peter 1:1). The American Standard Version more literally renders it, "to the elect who are sojourners of the Dispersion in Pontus, . . ." that is, to Jews who are absent from Palestine, residing in Gentile lands (cf. John 7:35). But care needs to be taken that the term *sojourners* be not limited to its literal force, but rather be given also its figurative meaning and spiritual application. It refers not strictly to the fleshly descendants of Abraham, but rather to his *spiritual* seed, who were partakers of the heavenly calling, and as such, were away from their home. The patriarchs "confessed that they were strangers and pilgrims on the earth. . . . For they . . . declare plainly that they seek a country . . . a better country [than the earthly Canaan], that is, an heavenly" (Heb. 11:13-16, brackets mine). Even David, while reigning as king in Jerusalem, made a similar acknowledgment: "I am a stranger in the earth" (Ps. 119:19). All Christians are strangers in this world; for while they are "at home in the body," they are "absent from the Lord" (II Cor. 5:6). Their citizenship is in heaven (Phil. 3:20). Thus it was spiritual sojourners (temporary residents) to whom Peter wrote, those who had been begotten to an inheritance reserved for them in heaven (I Peter 1:4).

Nor were all the spiritual strangers from the natural stock of Abraham. There is more than one indication in this very Epistle that while possibly a majority of them were Jewish believers, yet by no means were all of them so. Thus, in chapter 2, verse 10, after stating that God had called them out of darkness into His marvellous light, the Apostle Peter goes on to describe them with these words: "Which in time past were not a people, but are now the people of God: which had not obtained mercy, but now have obtained mercy." This precisely delineates the case of the *Gentile* believers (cf. Eph. 2:12, 13). Peter is here quoting from Hosea 1:9, 10 (where the "children of Israel" in v. 10 refers to the *spiritual* Israel), which is definitely interpreted for us in Romans 9:24, 25: "Even us, whom he hath called, not of the Jews only, but also of the Gentiles[.] As he saith also in Osee [Hosea], I will call them my people, which were not my people; . . ." (brackets mine). Again, in chapter 4, verse 3, Peter says by way of reminder to those to whom he is writing, "For the time past of our life may suffice us to have wrought the will of the Gentiles, when we walked in lasciviousness, lusts, excess of wine, revellings, banquetings, and abominable idolatries." The last category of transgression could only refer to Gentiles; for the Jews (when considered as a nation), since the Babylonian captivity, had never fallen into idolatry.

The Prayer Itself

As we examine together the prayer contained in I Peter 1:3-5, let us consider eight things: (1) its connection—that we may perceive who all are included by the words "begotten *us* again"; (2) its nature—a doxology ("Blessed be"); (3) its Object—"the God and Father of our Lord Jesus Christ"; (4) its ascription—"His abundant mercy"; (5) its incitement—"hath begotten us again unto a lively hope"; (6) its acknowledgment—"by the resurrection of Jesus Christ from the dead"; (7) its substance—"to an inheritance incorruptible, and undefiled, and that fadeth not away, reserved in heaven for you"; and (8) its guaranty—"who are kept by the power of God through faith." There is much here of interest and deep importance. Therefore, it would be wrong for us to hurriedly dismiss such a passage with a few generalizations, especially since it contains such a wealth of spiritual, joyful reflection that cannot but edify the mind and stir up the will and affections of every saint who rightly meditates upon it. May we be duly affected by its contents and truly enter into its elevated spirit.

First, we consider *its connection*. Those on whose behalf the apostle offered this doxology are spoken of according to their literal and figurative circumstances in verse 1, and then described by their spiritual characters: "Elect according to the foreknowledge of God the Father, through sanctification of the Spirit, unto obedience and sprinkling of the blood of Jesus Christ" (v. 2). That description pertains equally to *all* the regenerate in every age. When connected with election, the "foreknowledge of God" refers not to His eternal and universal prescience, for that embraces all beings and events, past, present and future; and, therefore, it has for its objects the non-elect as well as the elect. Consequently, there is no allusion whatever to God's preview of our believing or any other virtue in the objects of His choice. Rather, the term *foreknowledge* has respect to the spring or source of election, namely, God's unmerited good will and approbation. For this sense of the word *know* see the following: Psalm 1:6; Amos 3:2; II Timothy 2:19. For a like sense of the word *foreknow* see Romans 11:2. Therefore, the phrase "elect according to the foreknowledge of God" signifies that the favored persons thus described were fore-loved by Him, that they were the objects of His eternal favor, unalterably delighted in by Him as He foreviewed them in Christ— "wherein he hath made us accepted [or "objects of grace"] in the beloved" (Eph. 1:4-6, brackets mine).

Obedience, an Indispensable Sign of the Spirit's Saving Work

"Through sanctification of the Spirit." It is by means of the Spirit's gracious and effectual operations that our election by God the Father takes effect (see II Thess. 2:13). The words "sanctification of the Spirit" have reference to His work of regeneration, whereby we are quickened (made alive), anointed, and consecrated or set apart to God. The underlying idea of sanctification is almost always that of *separation*. By the new birth we are distinguished from those dead in sin. The words "unto obedience" here in I Peter 1:2 signify that by the Spirit's effectual call we are made subject to the authoritative call of the Gospel (see v. 22 and Rom. 10:1, 16) and subsequently to its precepts. Election never promotes license, but always produces holiness and good works (Eph. 1:4; 2:10). The Spirit regenerates sinners to a new life of hearty submission to Christ and not to a life of self-pleasing. When the Spirit sanctifies a soul, it is to the end that he may adorn the Gospel by a walk that is regulated thereby. It is by his obedience that a Christian makes evident his election by the Father, for previously he was one of "the children of disobedience" (Eph. 5:6). By his new life of obedience he furnished proof of the Spirit's supernatural work within him.

"And sprinkling of the blood of Jesus Christ." It is important for us to grasp the distinction between the sprinkling of Christ's blood and the shedding of it (Heb. 9:22). The *shedding* is Godward; whereas the *sprinkling* is its application to the believer, whereby he obtains forgiveness and peace of conscience (Heb. 9:13, 14; 10:22), and by which his service is rendered acceptable to God (I Peter 2:5).

A careful reading of the whole Epistle makes it evident that these saints were passing through severe trials (see I Peter 1:6, 7; 2:19-21; 3:16-18; 4:12-16; 5:8, 9). Jewish Christians (who evidently made up the majority of those originally addressed by Peter) have ever been sorely oppressed, persecuted not so much by the profane world as by their own brethren according to the flesh. How bitter and fierce was the hatred of such unbelieving Jews appears not only from the case of Stephen, but from what the Apostle Paul suffered at their hands (II Cor. 11: 24-26). As a means of encouragement, the Apostle Paul deliberately reminded his Hebrew brethren of the persecutions they had already endured for Christ's sake. "But call to remembrance the former days, in which, after ye were illuminated, ye endured a great fight of afflictions; . . . and took joyfully the spoiling of your goods" (Heb. 10:32-34). By bearing this fact in mind a better understanding is had of many of the details of the Book of Hebrews. Furthermore, it becomes more apparent why Peter has so much to say upon affliction, and why he refers so often to the sufferings of Christ. His brethren were in need of a stimulating cordial that would nerve them to heroic endurance. He therefore dwelt on those aspects of Divine truth best adapted to support the soul, strengthen faith, inspire hope, and produce steadfastness and good works.

This Prayer a Doxology, an Expression of Unmixed Praise to God

Secondly, we examine *its nature*. It is a tribute of praise. In this prayer the apostle is not making supplication to God, but rather is offering adoration to Him! This is as much our privilege and duty as it is to spread our needs before Him; yea, the one should ever be accompanied by the other. It is "with thanksgiving" that we are bidden to let our "requests be made known unto God" (Phil. 4:6). And that is preceded by the exhortation, "Rejoice in the Lord alway," which rejoicing is to find its expression in gratitude and by the ascribing of glory to Him. If we be suitably affected by God's bounties, we cannot but bless the Bestower of them. In verse 2, Peter had mentioned some of the most noteworthy and comprehensive of all the Divine benefits, and this exclamation, "Blessed be the God and Father of our Lord Jesus Christ!" is the echo, or better, the reflex of the Apostle Peter's heart in response to God's amazing grace toward himself and his brethren. This particular doxology is also to be regarded as a devout acknowledgment of the inestimable favors that God had bestowed on His elect, as enlarged upon in verse 3. As the apostle reflected upon the glorious blessings conferred on hell-deserving sinners, his heart was drawn out in fervent worship to the benign Author of them.

Thus it should be, thus it must be, with Christians today. God has no dumb children (Luke 17:7). Not only do they cry to Him day and night in their distress, but they frequently praise Him for His excellency and give thanks for His benefits. As they meditate upon His abundant mercy in having begotten them to a living hope, as they anticipate by faith the glorious inheritance that is reserved for them in heaven, and as they realize that these flow from the sovereign favor of God to them through the death and resurrection of His dear Son, well may they exclaim, "Blessed be the God and Father of our Lord Jesus Christ!" Doxologies, then, are expressions of holy joy and adoring homage. Concerning the particular term *blessed*, Ellicott most helpfully remarks,

> This form of Greek word is consecrated to God alone: Mark 14:61; Romans 9:5; II Corinthians 11:31. It is a completely different word from the "blessed" or "happy" of the Beatitudes and different from the "blessed" of our Lord's mother in Luke 1:28, 42. This form of it [in I Peter 1:3] implies that blessing is always *due* on account of something inherent in the person, while that only implies a blessing has been *received*.

Thus we see again how minutely discriminating and accurate is the language of Holy Writ.

The Glorious Object of Praise

Thirdly, we behold *its Object*. This doxology is addressed to "the God and Father of our Lord Jesus Christ," which is explained by Calvin thus:

> For as formerly, by calling Himself the God of Abraham, He designed to mark the difference between Him and all fictitious gods; so after He has manifested Himself in His own Son, His will is, not to be known otherwise than in Him. Hence they who form their ideas of God in His naked majesty apart from Christ, have an idol instead of the true God, as the case is with the Jews and the Turks [that is, the Mohammedans, to which we may add the

Unitarians]. Whosoever, then, seeks really to know the only true God, must regard Him as the Father of Christ. . . .

Moreover, in Psalm 72:17, it is foretold of Christ that "men shall be blessed in him" and that "all nations shall call him blessed." Whereupon the sacred singer breaks forth into this adoring praise: "Blessed be the LORD God, the God of Israel, who only doeth wondrous things" (v. 18). That was the Old Testament form of doxology (cf. I Kings 1:48; I Chron. 29:10); but the New Testament doxology (II Cor. 1:3; Eph. 1:3) is expressed in accordance with the self-revelation the Deity has made in the Person of Jesus Christ: "He that honoureth not the Son honoureth not the Father which hath sent him" (John 5:23).

God the Father is not here viewed absolutely but relatively, that is, as the God and Father of our Lord Jesus Christ. Our Lord Himself is contemplated in His mediatorial character, that is, as the eternal Son vested with our nature. As such, the Father appointed and sent Him forth on His redeeming mission. In that capacity and office the Lord Jesus owned and served Him as His God and Father. From the beginning He was engaged in His Father's business, ever doing those things that were pleasing in His sight. By God's Word He was regulated in all things. Jehovah was His "portion" (Ps. 16:5), His "God" (Ps. 22:1), His "All." Christ was under Him (John 6:38; 14:28): "the head of Christ is God" (I Cor. 11:3). In a covenant way, too, He was and is the God and Father of Christ (John 20:17), not only so while Christ was here on earth, but even now that He is in heaven. This is clear from Christ's promise after His ascension: "Him that overcometh will I make a pillar in the temple of *my God*, and he shall go no more out: and I will write upon him the name of my God . . ." (Rev. 3:12, ital. mine). Yet this *official* subordination of Christ to God the Father in no wise militates against nor modifies His essential equality with Him (John 1:1-3; 5:23; 10:30-33).

Because the Father of Our Surety, He Is Our Father

It is to be carefully noted that praise is here rendered not to "the God and Father of *the* Lord Jesus Christ" but of "*our* Lord Jesus Christ." In other words, God's relationship to us is determined by His relationship to our Surety. He is the God and Father of sinners only in Christ. He is adored as the covenant Head of the Savior and of His elect in Him. This is a point of first importance: the connection that the Church sustains to God is fixed by that of the Redeemer to God, for she is Christ's and Christ is God's (I Cor. 3:23). The title "God and Father of our Lord Jesus Christ" is the peculiar and characteristic *Christian* designation of Deity, contemplating Him as the God *of redemption* (Rom. 15:6; II Cor. 11:31; Col. 1:3). When an Israelite called on Him as "the God of Abraham, Isaac and Jacob," he recognized and owned Him not only as the Creator and moral Governor of the world, but also as the covenant God of his nation. So when the Christian addresses Him as "the God and Father of our Lord Jesus Christ," he acknowledges Him as the Author of eternal redemption through the incarnate Son, who voluntarily took the place of subserviency to and dependence upon Him. In the highest meaning of the word, God is the *Father* of no man until he is united to the One whom He commissioned and sent to be the Savior of sinners, the sole Mediator between God and men.

The language in which God is here worshiped *explains* how it is that He can be so kind and bounteous to His people. All blessings come to the creature from God. He it is who gave them being and supplies their varied needs. Equally so, all spiritual blessings proceed from Him (Eph. 1:3; James 1:17). The Highest is "kind unto the un-thankful and to the evil" (Luke 6:35). But spiritual bless-ings issue from Him not simply as God, nor from the Father absolutely, but from "the God and Father of our Lord Jesus Christ." In what follows, the apostle makes mention of His abundant mercy, of His begetting the elect to a living hope, and of an inheritance that infinitely tran-scends all earthly good. And in the bestowment of these favors God is here acknowledged in the special character in which He confers them. If it be asked, How can a holy God endow sinful men with such blessings? the answer is, as "the God and Father of our Lord Jesus Christ." It is because God is well pleased with the Redeemer that He is well pleased with the redeemed. The work of Christ merited such a reward, and He shares it with His own (John 17:22). All comes to us from the Father through the Son.

His Abundant Mercy, the Cause of God's Gracious Choice

Fourthly, let us ponder *its ascription*, which is found in the phrase "his abundant mercy." Just as God did not elect because He foresaw that any would savingly repent and believe the Gospel—for these are the effects of His invincible call, which in turn is *the consequence* and not the cause of election—but "according to his own purpose" (II Tim. 1:9), neither does He regenerate because of any merits possessed by the subjects thereof, but solely of His own sovereign pleasure (James 1:18). His abundant mercy is here set over against our abundant demerits, and to the degree that we are sensible of the latter shall we be moved to render praise for the former. Such is our woeful case through sin that naught but Divine mercy can relieve it. Give ear to the words of C. H. Spurgeon:

> No other attribute could have helped us had mercy refused. As we are by nature, justice condemns us, holiness frowns upon, power crushes us, truth confirms the threatening of the law, and wrath fulfils it. It is from the mercy of God that all our hopes begin. Mercy is needed for the miserable, and yet more for the sinful. Misery and sin are fully united in the human race, and mercy here performs her noblest deeds. My brethren, God has vouchsafed His mercy unto us, and we must thankfully acknowledge that in our case His mercy has been *abundant* mercy.
>
> We were defiled with abundant sin, and only the multitude of His loving kindnesses could have put those sins away. We were infected with an abundant evil, and only overflowing mercy can ever cure us of all our natural disease, and make us meet for heaven. We have received abundant grace up till now; we have made great drafts upon the exchequer of God, and of His fullness have all we received grace for grace. Where sin hath abounded, grace hath much more abounded. . . . Everything in God is on a grand scale. Great power—He shakes the world. Great wisdom—He balances the clouds. His mercy is commensurate with His other attributes: it is Godlike mercy, infinite mercy! You must measure His Godhead before you can compute His mercy. Well may it be called "abundant" if it be infinite. It will always be abundant, for all that can be drawn from it will be but as the drop of a bucket to the sea itself. The mercy which deals with us is not man's mercy, but God's mercy, and therefore boundless mercy.

5

I Peter 1:3-5

Part 2

"Blessed be the God and Father of our Lord Jesus Christ, which according to his abundant mercy hath begotten us again unto a lively hope." Let us begin this chapter with a continuation of our examination of the *ascription* of this doxology. God the Father is here viewed as the covenant Head of the Mediator and of God's elect in Him, and is thus accorded His distinctive *Christian* title (see, for example, Eph. 1:3). This title sets Him forth as the God of redemption. "Abundant mercy" is ascribed to Him. This is one of His ineffable perfections, yet the *exercise* of it—as of all His other attributes—is determined by His own imperial will (Rom. 9:15). Much is said in Scripture concerning this Divine excellency. We read of His "tender mercy" (Luke 1:78). David declares, "For great is thy mercy" (Ps. 86:13); "thou, Lord, art . . . plenteous in mercy" (Ps. 86:5). Nehemiah speaks of His "manifold mercies" (Neh. 9:27). Listen to David describe the effect that meditating upon this attribute, as he had practically experienced it, had upon his worship: "But as for me, I will come into thy house in the multitude of thy mercy: and in thy fear will I worship toward thy holy temple" (Ps. 5:7). Blessed be His name, "for his mercy endureth for ever" (Ps. 107:1). Well then may each believer join with the Psalmist in saying, "I will sing aloud of thy mercy . . ." (Ps. 59:16). To this attribute especially should erring saints look: "according unto the multitude of thy tender mercies blot out my transgressions" (Ps. 51:1).

God's General and Special Mercy Must Be Distinguished

It must be pointed out that there is both a general and a special mercy. That distinction is a necessary and important one, yea, a vital one; for many poor souls are counting upon the former instead of looking by faith to the latter. "The LORD is good to all: and his tender mercies are over all his works" (Ps. 145:9). Considering how much wickedness abounds in this world, the discerning and contrite heart can say with the Psalmist, "The earth, O LORD, is full of thy mercy . . ." (Ps. 119:64). For the good of our souls it is essential that we grasp the distinction revealed in God's Word between this general mercy and God's special benignity to His elect. By virtue of His eminence as a gift of God, Christ is denominated *"the Mercy* promised to our fathers" (Luke 1:72, ital. mine). How aptly does the Psalmist declare, "Thy mercy is great above the heavens" (Ps. 108:4; cf. Eph. 4:10); for there is God's mercyseat found (see Heb. 9, especially vv. 5, 23, 24), upon which the exalted Savior is now seated administering the fruits of His redemptive work. It is thither that the convicted and sin-burdened soul must look for saving mercy. To conclude that God is too merciful to damn any one eternally is a delusion with which Satan fatally deceives multitudes. Pardoning mercy is obtainable only through faith in the atoning blood of the Savior. Reject Him, and Divine condemnation is inescapable.

This Mercy Is Abundant Because It Is Covenant Mercy

The mercy here celebrated by Peter is very clearly a particular and discriminating one. It is that of "the God and Father of our Lord Jesus Christ," and it flows to its favored objects "by [means of] the resurrection of Jesus Christ from the dead." (brackets mine) It is between those two phrases that we find these words firmly lodged: "who according to his abundant mercy hath begotten us again unto a lively hope." Thus it is covenant mercy, redemptive mercy, regenerating mercy. Rightly is it styled "abundant mercy," especially in view of the Bestower. For this abundant mercy issues from the self-sufficient Jehovah, who is infinitely and immutably blessed in Himself, who would have incurred no personal loss had He abandoned the whole human race to destruction. It was of His mere good pleasure that He did not. It is seen to be "abundant mercy" when we view the character of its objects, namely, depraved rebels, whose minds were enmity against God. It also appears thus when we contemplate the nature of its peculiar blessings. They are not the common and temporal ones, such as health and strength, sustenance and preservation that are bestowed upon the wicked, but spiritual, celestial, and everlasting benefits such as had never entered the mind of man to conceive.

Still more so is it seen to be "abundant mercy" when we contemplate *the means* through which those blessings are conveyed to us: "by the resurrection of Jesus Christ from the dead," which necessarily presupposes His incarnation and crucifixion. What other language but "abundant mercy" could appropriately express the Father's sending forth of His beloved Son to take upon Himself the form of a servant, to assume to Himself flesh and blood, and to be born in a manger all for the sake of those whose multitudinous iniquities deserved eternal punishment? That Blessed One came here to be the Surety of His people, to pay their debts, to suffer in their stead, to die the Just for the unjust. Therefore, God spared not His own Son but called upon the sword of justice to smite Him. He delivered Him up to the curse that He might "freely give us all things" (Rom. 8:32). Thus it is a *righteous* mercy, even as the Psalmist declares: "Mercy and truth are met together; righteousness and peace have kissed each other" (Ps. 85:10). It was at the cross that the seemingly conflict-ing attributes of mercy and justice, love and wrath, holi-ness and peace united, just as the various colors of the light, when separated by a natural prism of mist, are seen beautifully blended together in the rainbow—the token and emblem of the covenant (Gen. 9:12-17; Rev. 4:3).

Meditation on the Miracle of the New Birth Evokes Fervent Praise

Fifthly, let us consider *the incitement* of this doxology, which is found in the following words: "which [who] ac-cording to his abundant mercy hath begotten us again unto a lively hope." It was the realization that God had quickened those who were dead in sins that moved Peter to bless Him so fervently. The words "hath begotten us" have reference to their regeneration. Later in the chapter the apostle describes them as having been "born again" (v. 23) and in the next chapter addresses them as "new-born babes" (I Peter 2:2). A new and a spiritual life, Divine in its origin, was imparted to them, wrought in their souls by the power of the Holy Spirit (John 3:6). That new life was given for the purpose of forming a new character and for the transforming of their conduct. God had sent forth the Spirit of His Son into their hearts, thereby communicating to them a holy disposition, who, as *the Spirit of adoption* (Rom. 8:15), was inclining them to love Him. It is styled a *begetting*, not only because it is then that the spiritual life begins and that a holy seed is implanted (I John 3:9), but also because an image or likeness of the Begetter Himself is conveyed (I John 5:1). As fallen Adam "begat a son in his own likeness, after his image" (Gen. 5:3), so at the new birth the Christian is "renewed in knowledge after the image of him that created him" (Col. 3:10).

In the words "begotten us *again*" there is a twofold allusion: a comparison and a contrast. First, just as God is the efficient cause of our being, so He is also of our well-being; our natural life comes from Him, and so too does our spiritual life. Secondly, the Apostle Peter intends to distinguish our new birth from the old one. At our first begetting and birth we were conceived in sin and shapen in iniquity (Ps. 51:5); but at our regeneration we are "created in righteousness and true holiness' (Eph. 4:24). By the new birth we are delivered from the reigning power of sin, for we are then made "partakers of the divine nature" (II Peter 1:4). Henceforth there is a perpetual conflict within the believer. Not only does the flesh lust against the spirit, but the spirit lusts against the flesh (Gal. 5:17). It is not sufficiently recognized and realized that the new nature or principle of grace of necessity makes war upon the old nature or principle of evil. This spiritual begetting is attributed to God's "abundant *mercy*," for it was induced by nothing in or from us. We had not so much as a desire after Him: in every instance He is able to declare, "I am found of them that sought me not" (Isa. 65:1; cf. Rom. 3:11). As believers love Him because He first loved them (I John 4:19), likewise they did not become seekers after Christ until He first sought and effectually called them (Luke 15; John 6:44; 10:16).

This begetting is according to the *abundant* mercy of God. Mercy was most eminently displayed here. For regeneration is the fundamental blessing of all grace and glory, being the first open manifestation that the elect receive of God's love to them. "But after that the kindness and love of God our Saviour toward man appeared, Not by works of righteousness which we have done, but according to his mercy he saved us, by the washing of regeneration, and renewing of the Holy Ghost" (Titus 3:4, 5). As Thomas Goodwin so aptly expressed it,

> God's love is like a river or spring which runs underground, and hath done so from eternity. When breaks it forth first? When a man is effectually called, then that river, which hath been from everlasting underground, and through Christ on the cross, breaks out in a man's own heart, too.

It is then that we are experientially made God's children, received into His favor, and conformed to His image. Therein is a remarkable display of His benignity. At the new birth the love of God is shed abroad in the heart, and that is the introduction into, as well as the sure pledge of, every other spiritual blessing for time and eternity. As the predestinating love of God ensures our effectual call or regeneration, so regeneration guarantees our justification and glorification (Rom. 8:29, 30).

God's Work of Regeneration Precedes Our Repentance and Faith

Let us now retrace our steps, going over again the ground we have covered, but in the inverse order. Not until a soul has been begotten of God can we have any spiritual apprehension of the Divine mercy. Before that miracle of grace takes place he is possessed more or less of a pharisaical spirit. To sincerely bless the God and Father of our Lord Jesus Christ for His abundant mercy is the heartfelt acknowledgment of one who has turned away with loathing from the filthy rags of his own righteousness (Isa. 64:6) and who places no confidence in the flesh (Phil. 3:3). Equally true is it that no unregenerate person ever has his conscience sprinkled with the peace-producing blood of Christ, for until spiritual life is imparted evangelical repentance and saving faith are morally impossible. Therefore, there can be no realization of our desperate need of a Savior or any actual trusting in Him until we are quickened (made alive) by the Holy Spirit (Eph. 2:1), that is, born again (John 3:3). Still more evident is it that so long as a person remains dead in sin, with his mind set at enmity against God (Rom. 8:7), there can be no acceptable obedience to Him; for He will neither be imposed upon nor bribed by rebels. And certain it is that none who are in love with this world's painted baubles will conduct themselves as "strangers and pilgrims on the earth"; for they are perfectly at home here.

Regeneration Produces a Living Hope

"Begotten us again unto a lively hope." This is the immediate effect and fruit of the new birth, and is one of the characteristic marks that distinguishes the regenerate from the unregenerate. Hope always has respect to something in the future (Rom. 8:24, 25), being an eager expectation of something desirable, an anticipation of a promised good, whether real or imaginary. The heart of the natural man is largely buoyed up, and his spirits maintained, by contemplations of some improvement in his lot that will increase his happiness in this world. But in the majority of instances the things dreamed of never materialize, and even when they do the result is always disappointing. For no real satisfaction of soul is to be found in anything under the sun. If such disillusioned souls have come under the influence of man-made religion, then they will seek to persuade themselves of, and look forward to, something far better for themselves in the hereafter. But such expectations will prove equally vain, for they are but the fleshly imaginings of carnal men. The false hope of the hypocrite (Job 8:13), the presumptuous hope of those who neither revere God's holiness nor fear His wrath but who count upon His mercy, and the dead hope of the graceless professor will but mock their subjects.

The Christian's Hope Is Both Living and Lively

In contradistinction to the delusive expectations cherished by the unregenerate, God's elect are begotten again to a real and substantial hope. This hope, which fills their minds and acts upon their wills and affections (thus radically altering the orientation of their thoughts, words, and deeds) is based upon the objective promises of God's Word (which are summarized in v. 4). In most of its occurrences, the Greek adjectival participle from *zaō* (to live; no. 2198 in Strong's Greek Dictionary) is translated *living*, though in Acts 7:38 (as here in I Peter 1:3) it is rendered *lively*. Both meanings are accurate and appropriate in this context. The Christian's hope is a sure and steadfast one (Heb. 6:19) because it rests upon the word and oath of Him that cannot lie. It is the gift of Divine grace (II Thess. 2:16), a fruit of the Spirit (Rom. 5:1-5), inseparably connected with faith and love (I Cor. 13:13). It is a living hope because it is exerted by a quickened soul, being an exercise of the new nature or principle of grace received at regeneration. It is a living hope because it has *eternal life* for its object (Titus 1:2). What a glorious change has taken place, for before we were begotten of God many of us were captivated by "a certain fearful looking for of judgment" (Heb. 10:27), and through fear of death were "all their [our] lifetime subject to bondage" (Heb. 2:15, brackets mine). It is also termed "a living hope" because it is imperishable, one that looks and lasts beyond the grave. Should death overtake its possessor, far from frustration, hope then enters into its fruition.

This inward hope of the believer is not only a living but a *lively* one, for it is—like faith and love—an active principle in his soul, animating him to patience, steadfastness, and perseverance in the path of duty. Therein it differs radically from the dead hope of religious formalists and empty professors, for theirs never stirs them to spiritual activity or produces anything to distinguish them from respectable worldlings who make no profession at all. It is the possession and exercise of this lively hope that affords demonstration that we have been "begotten . . . again." By Divine begetting a spiritual life is communicated, and that life manifests itself by desires after spiritual things, by a seeking of satisfaction in spiritual objects, and by a cheerful performance of spiritual duties. The genuineness and reality of this "lively hope" is, in turn, evidenced by its producing a readiness to the denying of self and to the enduring of afflictions, thus acting as "an anchor of the soul" (Heb. 6:19) amid the storms of life. This hope further distinguishes itself by purging its possessor. "And every man that hath this hope in him purifieth himself, even as he is pure" (I John 3:3). It is also a "lively hope" in that it cheers and enlivens its possessor;

for as he views the blissful goal courage is imparted and inspiration afforded, enabling him to endure to the end of his trials.

The Saving Virtue of Christ's Resurrection

Sixthly, let us consider *the acknowledgment* of this prayer, namely, "the resurrection of Jesus Christ." From the position occupied by these words, it is plain that they are related to and govern the preceding words as well as the verse that follows. Equally obvious it is that the resurrection of Christ implies His previous life and death, though each possesses its own distinctive value and virtue. The connection between the resurrection of Christ and the exercise of the abundant mercy of God the Father in His bringing us from death to life, His putting into our hearts a living hope, and His bringing us into a glorious inheritance is a very real and intimate one. As such it calls for our devout attention. The Savior's rising again from the dead was the climacteric proof of the Divine origin of His mission and thus a ratification of His Gospel. It was the fulfillment of Old Testament prophecies concerning Him, and thus proved Him to be the promised Messiah. It was the accomplishment of His own predictions, and thus certified Him to be a true prophet. It determined the context between Him and the Jewish leaders. They condemned Him to death as an impostor, but by restoring the temple of His body in three days He demonstrated that they were liars. It witnessed to the Father's acceptance of His redemptive work.

There is, however, a much closer connection between the resurrection of Christ from the dead and the hope of eternal life that is set before His people. His emerging in triumph from the tomb furnished indubitable proof of the efficacy of His propitiatory sacrifice, by which He had put away the sins of those for whom it was offered. This being accomplished, by His resurrection Christ brought in an everlasting righteousness (Dan. 9:24), thus securing for His people the eternal reward due Him by His fulfillment of God's Law by His own perfect obedience. He who was delivered up to death for our offenses was raised again for our justification (Rom. 4:25). Attend to the words of John Brown (to whose commentary on I Peter I am greatly indebted):

> When God "brought again from the dead our Lord Jesus, that great shepherd of the sheep, by the blood of the everlasting covenant," He manifested Himself to be "the God of peace," the pacified Divinity. He "raised him from the dead, and gave him glory, that our faith and hope might be in himself" [I Peter 1:21]. Had Jesus not risen, "our faith had been in vain; we should have been still in our sins" [I Cor. 15:17], and without hope. But now that He is risen,
>
> > Our Surety freed, declares us free,
> > For whose offences He was seized;
> > In His release our own we see,
> > And joy to view Jehovah pleased.

But even this is not all. Our Lord's resurrection is to be viewed not only in connection with His death, but with the following glory. Raised from the dead, He has received "all power in heaven and on earth, that he may give eternal life to as many as the Father had given him." How this is calculated to encourage hope, may be readily apprehended. "Because he lives, we shall live also." Having the keys of death and the unseen world, He can and will raise us from the dead, and give us eternal life. He sits at the right hand of God. "Our life is hid with him in God; and when he who is our life shall appear, we shall also appear with him in glory." We are not yet in possession of the inheritance; but He, our Head and Representative, is. "We see not yet all things put under us; but we see him," the Captain of our salvation, "for the suffering of death crowned with glory and honour." The resurrection of Christ, when considered in reference to the death which preceded and the glory which followed it, is the grand means of producing and strengthening the hope of eternal life.

By faith we now behold Christ seated at the right hand of the Majesty on high, from whence He is administering all the outworking of that redemption which He has accomplished. "Him hath God exalted with his right hand to be a Prince and a Saviour, for to give repentance to [the spiritual] Israel, and forgiveness of sins" (Acts 5:31, brackets mine).

More specifically, not only is the resurrection of Christ the legal basis upon which God the Father imputes the righteousness of Christ to the accounts of believing sinners, but it is also the legal warrant upon which the Holy Spirit proceeds *to regenerate* those sinners in order that they might initially believe on Christ, turn from their sins, and be saved. Unfortunately, like so many other fine points of Gospel doctrine, this is little understood today. The spirit of a man must be brought forth from its death in sin before his body will be subject to being raised in glory at the last day. And while the Holy Spirit is the One who spiritually quickens God's elect, it must be remembered that He is sent forth, to do His saving work, by the kingly power of the risen Christ, to whom that authority was given as the reward of His finished work (Matt. 28:18; Acts 2:33; Rev. 3:1). In James 1:18, the new birth is traced back to the sovereign will of the Father. In Ephesians 1:19 and following, the new birth and its gracious consequences are attributed to the gracious operation of the

Spirit. Here in our text, while issuing from the abundant mercy of the Father, it is ascribed to the virtue of Christ's triumph over death. It is to be observed that Christ's own resurrection is termed a *begetting* of Him (Ps. 2:7; cf. Acts 13:33), while our spiritual resurrection is designated a *regeneration* (Titus 3:5). Christ is expressly called "the first begotten of the dead" (Rev. 1:5). This He is called because His resurrection marked a new beginning both for Him and for His people.

6

I Peter 1:3-5

Part 3

"**B**lessed be the God and Father of our Lord Jesus Christ, which according to his abundant mercy hath begotten us again unto a lively hope by the resurrection of Jesus Christ from the dead." Let us begin this chapter by continuing our consideration of the *acknowledgment* of the prayer. It is to be recalled that this Epistle is addressed to those who are *strangers*, scattered abroad (v. 1). Most appropriate, then, is this reference to the Divine begetting of God's elect, for it is by the Holy Spirit's gracious begetting that the elect are constituted strangers or sojourners (that is, temporary residents of this world), both in heart and in conduct. The Lord Jesus was a stranger here (Ps. 69:8), for He was the Son of God from heaven; and so, too, are His people, for they have His Spirit within them. How that understanding enhances this miracle of grace! Divine begetting is not merely a doctrine, but the actual communication to the soul of the very life of God (John 1:13). Formerly the Christian was both *in* and *of* the world, but now his "conversation [citizenship—A.S.V.] is in heaven" (Phil. 3:20, brackets mine). "I am a stranger in the earth" (Ps. 119:19) is henceforth his confession. To the soul renewed by God this world becomes a barren wilderness. For his heritage, his home, is on high, and therefore he now views the things of time and sense in a very different light.

The Great Interests of the Regenerate Soul Are Alien to this World

The chief interests of a truly born-again soul lie not in this mundane sphere. His affections will be set upon things above; and in proportion as they *are* so, his heart is detached from this world. Their strangerhood is an essential mark that distinguishes the saints from the ungodly. They who heartily embrace the promises of God are suitably affected by them (Heb. 11:13). One of the certain effects of Divine grace in the soul is to separate its possessor, both in spirit and in practice, from the world. His delight in heavenly things manifests itself in his being weaned from the things of earth, just as the woman at the well left her bucket behind when she had obtained from Christ the living water (John 4:28). Such a spirit constitutes him an alien among the worshipers of mammon. He is morally a foreigner in a strange land, surrounded by those who know him not (I John 3:1), because they know not his Father. Nor do they understand his joys or sorrows, not appreciating the principles and motives that actuate him; for their pursuits and pleasures are radically different from his. Nay, he finds himself in the midst of enemies who hate him (John 15:19), and there are none with whom he can have communion save the very few who "have obtained like precious faith" (II Peter 1:1).

But though there be nothing in this wilderness of a world for the Christian, he has been "begotten . . . again unto a living hope." Previously he viewed death with horror, but now he perceives that it will provide a blessed release from all sin and sorrow and open the door into Paradise. The principle of grace received at the new birth not only inclines its possessor to love God and to act in faith upon His Word, but it also disposes him to "look not at the things which are seen, but at the things which are not seen" (II Cor. 4:17, 18), inclining his aspirations away from the present toward his glorious future. Thomas Manton aptly declares, "The new nature was made for another world: it came from thence, and it carrieth the soul thither." *Hope* is an assured expectation of future good. While faith is in exercise, a vista of unclouded bliss is set before the heart, and hope enters into the enjoyment of the same. It is a *living* hope exercised within a *dying* environment, and it both supports and invigorates all of us who believe. While in healthy activity, hope not only sustains amid the trials of this life but lifts us above them. Oh, for hearts to be more engaged in joyous anticipations of the future! For such hopeful hearts will quicken us to duty and stimulate us to perseverance. In proportion to the intelligence and strength of our hope will we be delivered from the fear of death.

Union with Christ in His Resurrection, the Cause of Our Regeneration

A further word must now be said upon the relationship that the resurrection of Jesus Christ from the dead bears to the Father's begetting of us to this living hope. Christ's God-honoring work and triumphant emergence from the grave was the legal basis not only of the justification of His people, but of their regeneration also. Mystically, by virtue of their union with Christ in the mind and purpose of God, they were delivered from their death at the hands of the Law when their Surety arose from the dead. "But God, who is rich in mercy, for his great love wherewith he loved us, Even when we were dead in sins, hath quickened us *together with* Christ, (by grace ye are saved;) and hath raised us up together . . ." (Eph. 2:4-6, ital. mine). Those words refer to the corporate union of the Church with her Head and her judicial participation in His victory, and not to an individual experience. Nevertheless, since all the elect rose federally when their Representative arose, they must in due time be regenerated; since they have been made alive legally, they must in due course be quickened spiritually. Had not Christ risen, none had been quickened (I Cor. 15:17); but because He lives, they shall live also.

> Jesus lives, and so shall I.
> Death! thy sting is gone forever!
> He who deigned for me to die,
> Lives, the bands of death to sever.
> He [hath raised] me from the dust:
> Jesus is my Hope and Trust.

The life that is in the Head must be communicated to the members of His body.

The resurrection of Christ is the *virtual* cause of our regeneration. The Holy Spirit would not have been given unless Christ had conquered the last enemy (I Cor. 15:26) and gone to the Father: "Christ hath redeemed us from the curse of the law, being made a curse for us: . . . that we might receive the promise of the Spirit through faith" (Gal. 3:13, 14). Regeneration issues as truly from the virtue of Christ's resurrection as does our justification, which is the result of that saving faith in Christ that can only issue from a Spirit-renewed heart. He purchased for His people the blessed Spirit to raise them up to grace and glory. "Not by works of righteousness which we have done, but according to his mercy he saved us, by the washing of regeneration, and renewing of the Holy Ghost; Which he shed on us abundantly *through* Jesus Christ our Saviour" (Titus 3:5, 6, ital. mine). God the Father has shed the Holy Spirit upon us in regenerating power because of the merits of Christ's life, death, and *resurrection*, and in response to His mediation on our behalf. The Holy Spirit is here to testify of Christ to God's elect, to raise up faith in them toward Him in order that they "may abound in hope" (Rom. 15:12, 13). Our spiritual deliverance from the grave of sin's guilt, power, and pollution is as much owing to the efficacy of Christ's triumph over death as will be our physical vivification at His return. He is "the firstborn among many brethren" (Rom. 8:29), the very life of Christ being imparted to them when they are begotten again.

The Power that Raised Christ Physically Raises Sinners Spiritually

The resurrection of Christ is also the *dynamic prototype* of our regeneration. The same power put forth in raising Christ's body is employed in the recovering of our souls from spiritual death (Eph. 1:19, 20; 2:1). The Lord Jesus is designated "the first begotten of the dead" (Rev. 1:5) because His emerging from the grave was not only the pledge but the likeness of both the regeneration of the spirits of His people and the raising of their bodies in the last day. The similitude is obvious. Begetting is the beginning of a new life. When Christ was born into this world it was "in the likeness of sinful flesh" (Rom. 8:3). Though untouched by the taint of original sin (Luke 1:35) and undefiled by the pollution of actual transgressions,

He was clothed with infirmity because of imputed iniquity. But when He rose from Joseph's tomb in power and glory, it was in a body fitted for heaven. Likewise, at regeneration, we receive a nature that makes us meet for heaven. As God's raising of Christ testified to His being pacified by His sacrifice (Heb. 13:20), so by begetting us again He assures us of our personal interest therein. As Christ's resurrection was the grand proof of His Divine Sonship (Rom. 1:4), so the new birth is the first open manifestation of our adoption. As Christ's resurrection was the first step into His glory and exaltation, so regeneration is the first stage of our entrance into all spiritual privileges.

Glorification Is the Goal of Regeneration

Our seventh consideration in examining this doxology is *its substance*: "to an inheritance incorruptible, and undefiled, and that fadeth not away, reserved in heaven for you" (v. 4). Regeneration is for the purpose of glorification. We are begotten spiritually to two realities: a living hope in the present, and a glorious heritage in the future. It is by God's begetting that we obtain our title to the latter. Inheritances go by birth: "Except a man be born of water and of the Spirit, he cannot enter into the kingdom of God" (John 3:5). If not sons, then we cannot be heirs; and we must be born of God in order to become the children of God. But "if children, then heirs; heirs of God, and joint-heirs with Christ" (Rom. 8:17). Not only does begetting confer title, but it also guarantees the inheritance. Already the Christian has received the Spirit, "[who] is the earnest of our inheritance (Eph. 1:14, brackets mine). As Christ's part was to purchase the inheritance, so the Spirit's part is to make it known to the heirs; for "the things which God hath prepared for them that love him"

He "hath revealed them unto us by his Spirit" (I Cor. 2:9, 10). It is the Spirit's province to vouchsafe to the regenerate sweet foretastes of what is in store for them, to bring something of heaven's joy into their souls on earth.

The New Birth Fits Us Immediately for Heaven

Not only does Divine begetting give title to and ensure the heavenly inheritance, but it also imparts a *meetness* for the same. At the new birth a nature is imparted that is suited to the celestial sphere, that qualifies the soul to dwell for ever with the thrice-holy God (as is evident from his present communion with Him); and at the close of his earthly pilgrimage, indwelling sin (which now hinders his communion) dies with the body. It is all too little realized by the saints that at regeneration they are at once fitted for heaven. Many of them—to the serious diminution of their peace and joy—suppose that they must still pass through a process of severe discipline and refining before they shall be ready to enter the courts above. That is but another relic of Romanism. The case of the dying thief, who was taken immediately from his spiritual birthplace into Paradise, should teach them better. But it does not. So legalistic remains the tendency of the heart even of a Christian that it is very difficult to convince him that the very hour he was born again he was made as suitable for heaven as ever he would be though he remained on earth another century. How difficult it is for us to believe that no growth in grace or passing through fiery trials is essential to prepare our souls for the Father's house.

Nowhere does Scripture say that believers are ripened, meetened, or gradually fitted for heaven. The Holy Spirit expressly declares that God the Father has, "according to His abundant mercy ... begotten us again ... to an inheritance." What could be plainer? Nor does our text by any means stand alone. Christians have already been made "partakers of the divine nature" (II Peter 1:4), and what more can be needed to fit them for the Divine presence? Scripture emphatically declares, "Wherefore thou art no more a servant [slave], but a son; and if a son, then an heir of God through Christ" (Gal. 4:7, brackets mine). The inheritance is the child's birthright or patrimony. To speak of *heirs* not being eligible for an estate is a contradiction in terms. Our fitness for the inheritance lies alone in our being the children of God. If it be true that except a man be born again he cannot enter or see the kingdom of God, then, conversely, it necessarily follows that once he *has been* born again he *is* qualified for an entrance into and enjoyment of God's kingdom. All room for argument on this point is excluded by these words, which set forth one aspect of Paul's prayers of thanksgiving on behalf of the Colossians: "Giving thanks unto the Father, which *hath* made [past tense] us meet to be partakers of the inheritance of the saints in light" (Col. 1:12, ital. and brackets mine).

By Regeneration We Are Wedded to Christ

By regeneration we are made vitally one with Christ and thereby become *joint-heirs* with Him. The portion of the Bride is her participation in the portion of the Bridegroom. "And the glory which thou gavest me I have given them" (John 17:22), declares the Redeemer of His redeemed. This, too, needs stressing today, when so much error is parading itself as the truth. In their fanciful attempts to "rightly divide the Word," men have wrongly divided the family of God. Some Dispensationalists hold that not only is there a distinction of earthly privileges, but that the same distinctions will be perpetuated in the world to come; that the New Testament believers will look down from a superior elevation upon Abraham, Isaac and Jacob; that saints who lived and died before Pentecost will not participate in the glory of the Church or enter into the inheritance "reserved for us in heaven." To affirm that the saints of this Christian era are to occupy a higher position and to enjoy grander privileges than will those of previous ages is a serious and inexcusable mistake, for it clashes with the most fundamental teachings of Scripture concerning the purpose of the Father, the redemption of Christ, and the work of the Spirit, and repudiates the essential features of God's great salvation. Writing to the churches in Galatia, largely composed of Gentiles, the Apostle Paul declares, "Know ye therefore that they which are of faith, the same are the children of Abraham (Gal. 3:7). This text alone is sufficient to prove that God's way of salvation has never essentially changed.

All of God's elect are the common sharers of the riches of His wondrous grace, vessels whom He "afore prepared unto glory" (Rom. 9:23), whom He predestinated to be "conformed to the image of his Son" (Rom. 8:29). Christ acted as the Surety of the entire election of grace, and what His meritorious work secured for one of them it necessarily secured for all. The saints of all ages are fellow-heirs. Each of them was predestinated by the same Father (John 6:37; 10:16, 27-30; 17:2, 9-12, 20-24); each of them was regenerated by the same Spirit (Eph. 4:4), each of them looked to and trusted in the same Savior. Scripture knows of no salvation that does not issue in joint-heirship with Christ. Those to whom God gives His Son, namely, the whole company of His elect from Abel to the end of earth's history, He also freely gives *all* things (Rom. 8:32). That both Abraham and David were justified by faith is plain from Romans 4, and there is no higher destiny or more glorious prospect than that to which justification gives full title. The renewing work of the Holy Spirit is identical in every member of God's family: begetting them to, qualifying them for, a celestial heritage. All those who were effectually called by Him during the Old Testament era received "the promise of eternal inheritance" (Heb. 9:15). Heaven-born children must have a heavenly portion.

The Nature of Our Eternal Inheritance

"An inheritance incorruptible, and undefiled, and that fadeth not away, reserved in heaven for you." The heavenly portion reserved for the people of God is one that is agreeable to the new life received at regeneration, for it is a state of perfect holiness and happiness suited to spiritual beings who possess material bodies. Many and varied are the descriptions given in Scripture of the nature of our inheritance. In our text (v. 5) it is described as "the salvation ready to be revealed in the last time" (cf. Heb. 9:28), that is, salvation in its fullness and perfection that shall be bestowed upon the redeemed at Christ's glorious return. Our Lord Jesus describes it as His "Father's house" in which there "are many mansions," which Christ Himself is now preparing for His people (John 14:1, 2). The Apostle Paul refers to it as "the inheritance of the saints in *light*" (Col. 1:12, ital. mine), and to the future inhabitants of that glorious realm as "the *children of light*" (I Thess. 5:5, ital. mine). No doubt these expressions point to the moral perfection of Him in the blazing light of whose Presence (Isa. 33:13; I Tim. 6:13-16; Heb. 12:29; I John 1:5) all the saints shall one day dwell. Furthermore, they underscore the spotless purity that shall characterize each of those who shall "dwell in the house of the LORD for ever" (Ps. 23:6; cf. Dan. 12:3; Rev. 21:27). Paul further describes it as "a city which hath foundations, whose builder and maker is God" (Heb. 11:10), upon which the hopeful, believing eye of Abraham was fixed. He also calls it "a kingdom which cannot be moved" or "shaken" (Heb. 12:26-28; cf. Rev. 21:10-27).

The Apostle Peter refers to Christians as those whom God has "called . . . unto his eternal glory by Christ Jesus" (I Peter 5:10). Elsewhere, he calls our inheritance "the everlasting kingdom of our Lord and Saviour Jesus Christ" (II Peter 1:11). The Lord Jesus prayed, "Father, I will that they also, whom thou hast given me, be with me where I am; that they may behold my glory" (John 17:24). The glorified Christ, in His revelation to the Apostle John, describes the saints' inheritance as "the paradise of God" (Rev. 2:7), from which we may infer that Eden was but a shadow. Looking forward to this Paradise, David declares, "Thou wilt shew me the path of life: in thy presence is fulness of joy; at thy right hand there are pleasures for evermore" (Ps. 16:11).

The Significance of the Term *Inheritance*

In his commentary on I Peter, John Brown makes the following pertinent observations on the significance of the use of the term *inheritance*:

> The celestial blessedness receives here, and in many other passages of Scripture, the appellation of "the inheritance," for two reasons: to mark its gratuitous nature, and to mark its secure tenure.
>
> An inheritance is something that is not obtained by the individual's own exertions, but by the free gift or bequest of another. The earthly inheritance of the external people

of God was not given them because they were greater or better than the other nations of the earth. It was "because the LORD had a delight in them to love them" [Deut. 10:15]. "They got not the land in possession by their own sword, neither did their own right hand save them; but thy right hand, and thine arm, and the light of thy countenance, for thou hadst a favour unto them" [Ps. 44:3]. And the heavenly inheritance of the spiritual people of God is entirely the gift of sovereign kindness. "By grace are ye saved" [Eph. 2:5]; "eternal life is the gift of God, through Jesus Christ our Lord" [Rom. 6:23].

A second idea suggested by the figurative expression, "the inheritance," when used in reference to the celestial blessedness, is the security of the tenure by which it is held. No right is more indefeasible than the right of inheritance. If the right of the giver or bequeather be good, all is secure. The heavenly happiness, whether viewed as the gift of the Divine Father, or the bequest of the Divine Son, is "sure to all the seed." If the title of the claimant be but as valid as the right of the original proprietor, their tenure must be as secure as the throne of God and His Son.

The Excellence of Our Inheritance

The *excellence* of this inheritance or everlasting portion of the redeemed is described by four expressions. First, it is *incorruptible*, and thus it is like its Author "the uncorruptible God" (Rom. 1:23). All corruption is a change from better to worse, but heaven is without change or end. Hence the word *incorruptible* has the force of enduring, imperishable. Nor will it corrupt its heirs, as many a worldly inheritance has done. Secondly, it is *undefiled*, and thus like its Purchaser, who passed through this depraved world as uncontaminated as a sunbeam is unsullied though it shines on a filthy object (Heb. 7:26). All defilement is by sin, but no germ of it can ever enter heaven. Hence *undefiled* has the force of *beneficent*, incapable of injuring its possessors. Thirdly, it is *unfading*, and thus it is like the One who conducts us thither, "the *eternal* Spirit" (Heb. 9:14, ital. mine), the Holy Spirit, "a pure river of water of life" (Rev. 22:1). The word *undefiled* tells of this River's perennial and perpetual freshness; its splendor will never be marred nor its beauty diminished. Fourthly, the phrase *reserved in heaven* speaks of the location and security of our inheritance (see Col. 1:5; II Tim. 4:18).

As we consider the four descriptive expressions in verse 4, several characteristics of our inheritance come into view. To begin with, our inheritance is *indestructible*. Its substance is wholly unlike that of earthly kingdoms, the grandeur of which wears away. The mightiest empires of earth eventually dissipate by reason of inherent corruption. Consider the *purity* of our portion. No serpent shall ever enter this Paradise to defile it. Behold its changeless *beauty*. Neither rust shall tarnish nor moth mar it, nor shall endless ages produce a wrinkle on the countenance of any of its inhabitants. Ponder its *security*. It is guarded by Christ for His redeemed; no thief shall ever break into it.

It seems to me that these four expressions are designed to cause us to make a series of contrasts with the glorious inheritance that awaits us. First, consider the inheritance of Adam. How soon was Eden corrupted! Secondly, think of the inheritance that "the most High divided to the nations" (Deut. 32:8) and how they have defiled it by greed and bloodshed. Thirdly, contemplate the inheritance of Israel. How sadly the land flowing with milk and honey wilted under the droughts and famines that the Lord sent in order to chasten the nation for their sins. Fourthly, let us reflect on the glorious habitation that was forfeited by the fallen angels, who "kept not their first estate" (Jude 6). These woeful, benighted spirits have no gracious High Priest to intercede for them, but are "*reserved* in everlasting chains under darkness unto the judgment of the great day." Knowing our own remaining corruption, well might we shudder and ask with pious self-distrust (see Matt. 26:20-22), "What will *keep us* from such a doom?"

The Guarantee that We Will Receive Our Inheritance

We come, finally, to reflect upon the infallible *guaranty* of this doxology, which graciously answers the question of trembling saints just posited: "Who are *kept by the power of God* through faith unto salvation ready to be revealed at the last time." Here is the cordial for the fainting Christian! Not only is the inestimably glorious and precious inheritance secure, "reserved in heaven" for us, but *we also* are secure, "kept by the power of God." Here the Apostle Peter's doctrine perfectly coincides with that of the Lord Jesus and of the other apostles. Our Lord taught that those who are born or begotten of God believe on His Son (John 1:11-13; 3:3-5), and that those who believe *have* eternal life (John 3:15, 16). "He that believeth on the Son *hath* [presently and continually possesses] everlasting life" (John 3:36, ital. and brackets mine). He further taught that those who believe not *do not believe* because they are not His sheep (John 10:26). But then He goes on:

> My sheep hear my voice, and I know them, and they follow me: And I give unto them eternal life; and they shall never perish, neither shall any man pluck them out of my hand. My Father, which gave them me, is greater than all; and no man is able to pluck them out of my Father's hand. I and my Father are one (John 10:27-30).

The Apostle Paul also declares the fact that none of Christ's brethren shall ever perish.

> Who shall separate us from the love of Christ? shall trib-
> ulation, or distress, or persecution, or famine, or naked-
> ness, or peril, or sword? . . . Nay, in all these things we
> are more than conquerors through him that loved us. For
> I am persuaded, that neither death, nor life, nor angels,
> nor principalities, nor powers, nor things present, nor
> things to come, nor height, nor depth, nor any other crea-
> ture, shall be able to separate us from the love of God,
> which is in Christ Jesus our Lord (Rom. 8:35, 37-39).

Yet the question remains to be answered, "What is the principal means that the power of God exercises in preserving us, in order that we might enter upon and enjoy our inheritance?"

Faith Is the Means of Our Preservation

"Who are kept by the power of God *through faith*." John Brown's insights are of great value on this point:

> They are "kept"—preserved safe—amid the many dan-
> gers to which they are exposed, "by the power of God."
> The expression, "power of God," may here refer to the
> Divine power both as exercised in reference to the ene-
> mies of the Christian, controlling their malignant pur-
> poses, and as exercised in the form of spiritual influence
> on the mind of the Christian himself, *keeping him in
> the faith of the truth* [italics mine] "in the love of God,
> and in the patient waiting for our Lord Jesus Christ"
> [II Thess. 3:5; cf. II Tim. 1:13, 14]. It is probably to the
> last that the apostle principally alludes, for he adds "by
> faith." It is through the persevering faith of the truth that
> the Christian is by Divine influence preserved from fall-
> ing, and kept in possession both of that state and char-

acter which are absolutely necessary to the enjoyment of the heavenly inheritance.

The perseverance thus secured to the true Christian is perseverance in faith and holiness; and nothing can be more grossly absurd than for a person living in unbelief and sin to suppose that he can be in the way of obtaining celestial blessedness.

Though God Keeps Us, We Must Believe

By the almighty power of the Triune God, we are kept "unto salvation ready to be revealed in the last time." But the same gracious Spirit who keeps us also inspired Jude to write, "*Keep yourselves* in the love of God, looking for the mercy of our Lord Jesus Christ unto eternal life" (Jude 21, ital. mine). By Him also the Apostle Paul wrote, "Put on the whole armour of God, . . . Above all, taking the shield of faith, wherewith ye shall be able to quench all the fiery darts of the wicked" (Eph. 6:11, 16). Therefore ought we frequently to cry to the Lord with the apostles, "Increase our faith" (Luke 17:5). If our cry is genuine, then we may be certain that Jesus, who is "the author and finisher of our faith" (Heb. 12:2) will hear and answer in a way best suited to our need, though perhaps by means of adversity.

The apostle's reference to the heavenly heritage of believers was a most appropriate one. He was writing to those who were, both naturally and spiritually, away from their homeland, aliens in a strange country. Many of them were converted Jews, and, as such, fiercely opposed and most cruelly treated. When a Jew became a Christian he forfeited much: he was excommunicated from the synagogue, becoming an outcast from among his own people. Nevertheless, there was rich compensation for him. He had been Divinely begotten to an inheritance infinitely superior, both in quality and duration, to the land of Palestine. Thus his gains far more than made up for his losses (see Matt. 19:23-29, especially v. 29). The Holy Spirit, then, from the outset of the Epistle, drew out the hearts of those suffering saints to God by setting before them His abundant mercy and the exceeding riches of His grace. The more they were occupied with the same the more their minds would be lifted above this scene and their hearts filled with praise to God. While few of *us* are experiencing any trials comparable to *theirs*, yet our lot is cast in a very dark day, and it behooves us to look away from the things that are seen and more and more to fix our attention upon the blissful future awaiting us. Since God has designed such for us, how we should glorify Him in heartfelt worship and by adhering to His promises by "the obedience of faith" (Rom. 16:26) to the end!

7

I Peter 5:10, 11

Part 1

We come now to an apostolic prayer the contents of which, as a whole, are very sublime. Its contents are remarkably full, and a careful study of, and devout meditation upon, it shall be richly repaid. My present task will be rendered the easier since I am making extensive use of Thomas Goodwin's excellent and exhaustive exposition of the passage. He was favored with much light on this portion of Scripture, and I wish to share with my readers what has been of no little help and blessing to me personally.

There are seven things that we should consider regarding this prayer: (1) *the supplicant*, for there is an intimate and striking relationship between the experiences of Peter and the terms of his prayer; (2) *its setting*, for it is closely connected with the context, particularly with verses 6-9; (3) *its Object*, namely, "the God of all grace"—a title especially dear to His people and most appropriate in this context; (4) *its plea*, for so ought the clause "who hath called us into his eternal glory by Christ Jesus" to be regarded; (5) *its petition*, "make you perfect, stablish, strengthen, settle you"; (6) *its qualification*, "after that ye have suffered a while," for though that clause precedes the petition, yet it logically follows it when the verse is treated homiletically; and (7) *its ascription*, "to him be glory and dominion for ever and ever. Amen."

"But the God of all grace, who hath called us unto his eternal glory by Christ Jesus, after that ye have suffered a while, make you perfect, stablish, strengthen, settle you" (v. 10). In these words the apostle begins his appeal to Him who is the Fountain of grace, and with such a One to look to the chief of sinners need not despair. Next, he mentions that which gives proof to all believers that He is indeed the God of all grace, namely, His having effectually called them from death to life and having brought them out of nature's darkness into His own marvelous light. Nor is that all, for regeneration is but an earnest of what He has designed and prepared for them, since He has called them to His eternal glory. The realization of that truth moves the Apostle Peter to request that, following a season of testing and affliction, God would complete His work of grace within them. Herein we have it clearly implied that God will preserve His people from apostasy, will move them to persevere to the end, and, notwithstanding all the opposition of the world, the flesh, and the devil, will bring them safe to heaven.

The Supplicant's Experience of Restoring and Preserving Grace

First let us consider this prayer's *supplicant*. The one who approached God thus was Simon Peter. While Paul had much more to say about the grace of God than any other of the apostles, it was left to poor Peter to denominate Him "the God of all grace." We shall not have to seek far in order to discover the reason for this and its appropriateness. While Saul of Tarsus is the outstanding New Testament trophy of *saving* grace (for king Manasseh is an equally remarkable case in the Old Testament), surely it is Simon who is the most conspicuous New Testament example (David supplies a parallel under the Mosaic era) of the *restoring and preserving* grace of God. What is it that appears the greater marvel to a Christian, that most moves and melts his heart before God? Is it the grace shown to him while he was dead in sin, that which lifted him out of the miry clay and set him upon and within the Rock of ages? Or is it that grace exercised toward him *after* conversion that bears with his waywardness, ingratitude, departures from his first love, grievings of the Holy Spirit, dishonorings of Christ; and yet, notwithstanding all, loves him to the end and continues ministering to his every need? If the reader's experience be anything like mine, he will have no difficulty in answering.

Who but one who has been made painfully sensible of the plague within him, who has had so many sad proofs of the deceitfulness and desperate wickedness of his own heart, and who has perceived something of the exceeding sinfulness of sin—not only in the light of God's holiness but as it is committed against the dying love of his Savior—can rightly estimate the sad fall of Peter? For he was not only accorded a place of honor among the twelve ambassadors of the King of glory, but was privileged to behold Him on the mount of transfiguration, and was one of the three who witnessed more than any others His agonies in the Garden. And then to hear him, a very short time afterwards, denying his Master and Friend with oaths! Who but one who has personally experienced the "longsuffering of God" (I Peter 3:20; II Peter 3:9, 15), and has himself been the recipient of His "abundant mercy"

(I Peter 1:3), can really estimate and appreciate the amazing, infinite grace (1) that moved the Savior to look so sorrowfully yet tenderly upon the erring one as to cause him to go forth and "weep bitterly" (Luke 22:62), (2) that led Him to have a private interview with Peter after His resurrection (Luke 24:34; I Cor. 15:5), and (3) that, above all, not only recovered His wandering sheep but restored him to the apostolate (John 21:15-17)? Well might Peter own Christ, together with the Father and the Spirit, as "the God of *all* grace"!

The Twin Duties of Christian Pastors

Secondly, let us ponder the *setting* of this prayer, for if we closely examine it we shall find that there is much to be learned and admired. Before entering into detail, let us observe the context generally. In the foregoing verses the apostle had been making a series of weighty exhortations. And since those in verses 6 through 9 are preceded by Peter's impressing upon the public servants of God their several duties (vv. 1-4), allow me to address a word to them first. Let all Christ's undershepherds emulate the example that is here set before them. Having bidden believers to walk circumspectly, the apostle bent his knees and commended them to the gracious care of their God, seeking for them those mercies that he felt they most needed. The minister of Christ has two principal offices to discharge for those souls that are committed to his care (Heb. 13:17): to speak for God *to* them, and to supplicate God *for* them. The seed that the minister sows is not likely to produce much fruit unless he personally waters it with his prayers and tears. It is but a species of hypocrisy for him to exhort his hearers to spend more time in prayer if *he* be not a frequenter of the throne of grace. The pastor has only fulfilled half his commission when he has faithfully proclaimed all the counsel of God; the other part is to be performed in private.

The Twin Duties of Hearers and Students of God's Word

The same principle holds good equally for those in the pew. The most searching sermon will profit the hearer little or nothing unless it be turned into fervent prayer. So too with what we *read*! The measure in which God is pleased to bless these chapters to you will be determined by the influence they have upon you and the effects they produce in you—the extent to which they bring you to your knees in earnest supplication seeking power from the Lord. From exhortation the apostle turned to supplication. Let us do likewise, or we shall be left without the necessary strength to obey the precepts. To the various duties inculcated in the context was added this prayer for Divine enablement for the discharge of them, however arduous, and for the patient endurance of every trial, however painful. Observe, too, the blessed contrast between the assaults of the enemy in verses 8 and 9 and the character in which God is here viewed in verses 10 and 11. Is not that designed to teach the saint that he has nothing to fear from his vile adversary so long as he has recourse to Him in whom resides every kind of grace that is needed for his present walk, work, warfare, and witness? Surely this is one of the principal practical lessons to be drawn from this prayer as we view it in the light of its context.

Our Ability to Resist Satan Depends on Prayer

Unless we daily look to and cast ourselves upon "the God of all grace," it is certain that we shall never be able to "resist stedfast in the faith" our adversary the devil, who, "as a roaring lion, walketh about, seeking whom he may devour" (v. 8). And equally sure is it that Divine grace is needed by us if we are to "be sober, be vigilant." We need strengthening grace that we may successfully resist so powerful a foe as the devil; we need courage-producing grace if we are to do so steadfast in the faith; and we need patience-producing grace in order to meekly bear afflictions. Not only is every *kind* of grace available for us in God but every *measure*, so that when we find one exhausted we may obtain a fresh one. One of the reasons why God permits Satan to assail His people so frequently and so fiercely is that they may prove for themselves the efficacy of His grace. "And God is able to make all grace abound toward you; that ye, always having all sufficiency in all things, may abound to every good work" (II Cor. 9:8). Then let us bring to Him every pitcher of our needs and draw upon His inexhaustible fullness. Says F. B. Meyer, "The ocean is known by several names, according to the shores it washes, but it is the same ocean. So it is ever the same love of God, though each needy one perceives and admires its special adaptation to *his* needs."

The Remarkable Correspondence Between Peter's Experience and His Exhortation and Prayer

But, as Thomas Goodwin has shown, there is a yet more definite relation between this prayer and its context, and between both of them and the experience of Peter. The parallels between them are so close and numerous that they cannot be undesigned. In Gethsemane Christ bade His servant, "Watch and pray, that ye enter not into temptation" (Matt. 26:41), and in his Epistle Peter exhorts the saints, "be sober, be vigilant." Previously, the Savior had

warned him, "Simon, Simon, behold, Satan hath desired
to have you, that he may sift you as wheat" (Luke 22:31)—
and as the Puritan expressed it, "and shake forth all grace
out of him." So in verse 8 Peter gives point to his call for
sobriety and vigilance by saying, "because your adversary
the devil, as a roaring lion, walketh about, seeking whom
he may devour." But in connection with the loving ad-
monition Christ comforted him: "But I have prayed for
thee, that thy faith fail not" (Luke 22:32). As Goodwin
points out, "Faith's not failing is Satan's foiling." Likewise, the Apostle Peter, in his exhortation, adds, "Whom
resist stedfast in the faith"—the *gift* of faith, as Calvin
expounds it. Though Peter's self-confidence and courage
failed him, so that he fell, yet his faith delivered him from
giving way to abject despair, as Luke 22:61, 62, shows.

Our Lord concluded His address to Simon by saying,
"and when thou art converted [brought back, restored],
strengthen thy brethren" (Luke 22:32, brackets mine).
Likewise, our apostle wrote, "knowing that the same afflictions are accomplished in your brethren that are in the
world" (v. 9); and then he prayed that, after they had suffered awhile, the God of all grace would "perfect [or re-
store], stablish, strengthen, settle you [them]." He prayed
for the same kind of deliverance for them as that which
he himself had experienced. Finally, Goodwin observes
that Christ, when strengthening Peter's faith against Satan, set His "But I have prayed for thee" over against the
worst the enemy could do. Therefore Peter also, after portraying the adversary of the saints in his fiercest character—as "a roaring lion"—brings in by way of contrast
these words: "*But* the God of all grace, who hath called
us unto his eternal glory by Christ Jesus, after that ye
have suffered a while, make you perfect, stablish,
strengthen, settle you." He thereby assures them that God

will be their Guardian, Establisher, and Strengthener. If, notwithstanding his sad lapse, *he* was recovered and preserved to eternal glory, that is a sure pledge that *all* the truly regenerate will be also. How admirably Scripture (Luke 22) interprets Scripture (I Peter 5)!

God's Choice of Instruments for Writing His Scriptures Amazingly Appropriate

Before passing on to our next section, let us note and admire how the particular instruments whom God employs as His penmen in communicating His Word were personally qualified and experientially fitted for their several tasks. Who but Solomon was so well suited to write the Book of Ecclesiastes? For he was afforded exceptional opportunities to drink from all the poor cisterns of this world, and then to record the fact that no satisfaction was to be found in them. He thereby provided a fitting background for the Song of Solomon, wherein a Satisfying Object *is* displayed. How appropriate was the selection of Matthew to be the writer of the first Gospel, for he was the only one of the Twelve who held an official position before his call to the ministry (a tax-gatherer in the employ of the Romans). He of the four Evangelists presents Christ most clearly in His official character as the Messiah and King of Israel. Mark, the one who ministered to another (II Tim. 4:11), is the one chosen to set forth Christ as the servant of Jehovah. Who was so eminently adapted to write upon the blessed theme of Divine love (as he does throughout his Epistles) as the one who was so highly favored as to lean upon the bosom of God's Beloved? So here, *Peter* is the one who so feelingly styles the Deity "the God of all grace." And so it is today. When God calls any man to the ministry, He experientially equips him, qualifying him for the particular work He has for him to do.

That He Is "the God of All Grace" Is Uniquely a Gospel Truth

Thirdly, let us contemplate *its Object*: "The God of all grace." Nature does not reveal Him as such, for man has to work hard and earn what he obtains from her. The workings of Providence do not, for there is a stern aspect as well as a benign one to them; and, as a whole, they rather exemplify the truth that we reap as we sow. Still less does the Law, as such, exhibit God in this character, for its reward is a matter of debt and not of grace. It is only in the Gospel that He is clearly made manifest as "the God of all grace." Our valuation of Him as such is exactly proportioned by our devaluation of ourselves, for grace is the gratuitous favor of God to the undeserving and ill-deserving. Therefore we cannot truly appreciate it until we are made sensible of our utter unworthiness and vileness. He might well be the God of inflexible justice and unsparing wrath to rebels against His government. Such indeed He is to all who are outside of Christ, and will continue so for all eternity. But the glorious Gospel discovers to hell-deserving sinners the amazing grace of God to pardon, and to cleanse the foulest who repent and believe. Grace devised the plan of redemption; grace executed it; and grace applies it and makes it effectual. Peter previously made mention of "the *manifold* grace of God" (I Peter 4:10, ital. mine), for nothing less will avail for those who are guilty of "manifold transgressions" and "mighty sins" (Amos 5:12). The grace of God is manifold not only numerically but in *kind*, in the rich variety of its manifestations. Every blessing we enjoy is to be ascribed to grace. But the appellation "the God of *all* grace" is even more comprehensive; yea, it is incomprehensible to all finite intelligences. This title, as we have seen, is set over against what is said of the devil in verse 8, where he is portrayed in all his terribleness: as our *adversary* for malice; likened to a *lion* for strength; to a *roaring lion* for dread; described as *walking about* for unwearied diligence, "seeking whom he may devour" unless God prevent. How blessed and consolatory is the contrast: "But God"—the Almighty, the Self-sufficient and All-sufficient One—"the God of *all grace*." How comforting is the singling out of *this* attribute when we have to do with Satan in temptation! If the God of all grace be *for* us, who can be against us? When Paul was so severely tried by the messenger (angel) of Satan who was sent to buffet him, and he thrice prayed for its removal, God assured him of His relief: "My *grace* is sufficient for thee' (II Cor. 12:9, ital. mine).

The God of All Grace: A Great Encouragement to Prayer

Though mention is made frequently in the Scriptures of the grace of God and of His being gracious, yet nowhere but in this verse do we find him denominated "the God of all grace." There is a special emphasis here that claims our best attention: not simply is He "the God of grace," but "the God of *all* grace." As Goodwin showed, He is "the God of all grace" (1) essentially in His own character, (2) in His eternal purpose concerning His people, and (3) in His actual dealings with them. God's people personally receive constant proof that He is indeed so; and those of them whose thoughts are formed by His Word know that

the benefits with which He daily loads them are the out-
workings of His *everlasting design* of grace toward them.
But they need to go still farther back, or raise their eyes
yet higher, and perceive that all the riches of grace He
ordained, and of which they are made the recipients, are
from and in His very *nature*. "The grace in His nature is
the fountain or spring; the grace of His purposes is the
wellhead, and the grace in His dispensations the streams,"
says Goodwin. It was the grace of His nature that caused
Him to form "thoughts of peace" toward His people
(Jer. 29:11), as it is the grace in His heart that moves Him
to fulfil the same. In other words, the grace of His very
nature, what He is *in Himself*, is such that it guarantees
the making good of all His benevolent designs.

As He is the Almighty, self-sufficient and omnipotent,
with whom all things are possible, so He is also an all-
gracious God in Himself—lacking no perfection to make
Him infinitely benign. There is therefore a sea of grace in
God to feed all the streams of His purposes and dispensations that are to issue therefrom. Here then is our grand
consolation: all the grace there is in His nature, which
makes Him to be the "God of all grace" to His children,
renders certain not only that He will manifest Himself as
such to them, but guarantees the supply of their every
need and ensures the lavishing of the exceeding riches of
His grace upon them in the ages to come (Eph. 2:7). Look
then beyond those *streams* of grace of which you are now
the partaker to the God-man, Jesus the Anointed One,
who is "full of grace" (John 1:14), and ask for continual
and larger supplies from Him. The straitness is in ourselves and not in Him, for in God there is a boundless and
limitless supply. I beg you (as I urge myself) to remember
that when you come to the mercyseat (to make known
your requests) you are about to petition "the God of all

grace." In Him there is an infinite ocean to draw upon, and He bids you come to Him, saying, "open thy mouth *wide*, and I will fill it" (Ps. 81:10, ital. mine). Not in vain has He declared, "According to your faith be it unto you."

Only by Faith Can We Enjoy the God of All Grace

The Giver is greater than all His gifts, yet there must be a personal and appropriating *faith* in order for any of us to *enjoy Him*. Only thus can we particularize what is general. God is the God of all grace to *all* saints, but faith has to be individually directed toward God by *me* if I am to know and delight in Him for what He actually is. We have an example of this in Psalm 59, where David declared, "The God of *my mercy* shall prevent [or "anticipate"] me" (v. 10, ital. and brackets mine). There we find him appropriating God *to himself* personally. Observe, first, how David lays hold of the *essential* mercy of God, that mercy which is embedded in His very nature. He exults again in verse 17: "Unto thee, *O my strength*, will I sing: for God is my defence, and the God of my mercy" (ital. mine). The God of all grace is *my Strength*. He is *my God*, and therefore the God of *my mercy*. I lay claim to Him as such; all the mercy there is *in Him* is mine. Since He is my God, then *all* that is in Him is mine. It was, after all, the mercy and grace that are in Him that moved Him to set His love upon me and to enter into covenant with me, saying, "I will be his God, and he shall be my son" (Rev. 21:7). Says Goodwin:

> You [have] heard [it said], God is the God of all grace to the brotherhood; I tell thee, if any soul had all the needs that all the brotherhood have, if nothing would serve his turn, but all the grace of God that He hath for the whole,

yea, in the whole of Himself, He would lay it out for thee.
. . . Poor soul, thou usest to say, this or that is my sin, and
it is so; a grievous sin perhaps, and I am prone to it. And
again, this is my misery; but withal, I beseech thee to
consider, that God is the God of thy mercy, and that all
the mercy in God, upon occasion, and for a need, is thine,
and all upon as good a title as that sin is thine; for the
free donation of God, and of His will, is as good a title as
the inheritance of sin in thee.

Thus we see that God's mercy shall be employed on our
behalf in our hour of need as though each of us were His
only child. Just as surely as we had inherited the guilt
and miseries of Adam's transgressions have we, who are
in Christ, title to *all* of God's grace and mercy.

Furthermore, observe that David lays hold of the *purposing* mercy of God. Each individual saint has appointed
and allotted to him that which he may call "my mercy."
God has set apart in His decree a portion so abundant
that it can never be exhausted either by your sins or your
needs. "The God of all mercy shall prevent me." From all
eternity He has *anticipated* and made full provision in
advance for all my needs, just as a wise father has a med-
icine chest prepared with remedies for the ailments of his
children. "And it shall come to pass, that *before* they call,
I will answer; and while they are yet speaking, I will hear"
(Isa. 65:24, ital. mine). What an amazing condescension
it is that God should make this a characteristic of Himself,
that He becomes the God of the mercy of every particular
child of His!

Finally, let us lay hold of His *dispensing* mercy, that
which is actually bestowed upon us moment by moment.
Here, too, has the believer every occasion to say "The God
of my mercy," for every blessing enjoyed by me proceeds
from His hand. This is no empty title of His, for the fact

that David's use of it is recorded for us in Holy Writ ensures that He will make it good. When I use it in true faith and childlike dependence upon Him, He binds Himself to take care of my interests in every way. Not only is He my God personally, but also of my needs.

8

I Peter 5:10,11

Part 2

"**B**ut the God of all grace, who hath called us." In the last chapter (utilizing Goodwin's analysis) it was pointed out that this most blessed title has respect to what God is in Himself, what He is in His eternal purpose, and what He is in His actings toward His people. Here, in the words just quoted, we see the three things joined together in a reference to God's effectual *call*, whereby He brings a soul out of nature's darkness into His own marvelous light (I Peter 2:9). This special inward call of the Holy Spirit, which immediately and infallibly produces repentance and faith in its object, thus furnishes the *first* evident or outward proof that the new believer receives that God is in truth to him "the God of all grace." Though that was not the first outgoing of God's heart to him, nevertheless, it is the *proof* that His love had been set upon him from all eternity. "Moreover whom he did predestinate, them he also called" (Rom. 8:30). God has "from the beginning chosen you [His people] to salvation" (II Thess. 2:13, 14, brackets mine). In due time He brings about their salvation by the invincible operations of the

Spirit, who capacitates and causes them to believe the
Gospel. They believe through grace (Acts 18:27), for faith
is the gift of Divine grace (Eph. 2:8), and it is given them
because they belong to "the election of grace" (Rom. 11:5).
They belong to that favored election because the God of
all grace has, from eternity past, singled them out to be
the everlasting monuments of His grace.

Regeneration Is the Fruit of Election, Not Its Cause

That it was the grace that was in the heart of God that
moved Him to call us is clear from II Timothy 1:9: "Who
hath saved us, and called us with an holy calling, not
according to our works, but according to his own purpose
and grace, which was given us in Christ Jesus before the
world began." Regeneration (or effectual calling) is the
consequence, and not the cause, of Divine predestination.
God resolved to love us with an unchangeable love, and
that love designed that we should be partakers of His
eternal glory. His good will toward us moves Him so infallibly to carry out all the resolutions of His free grace
toward us that nothing can thwart it, though in the exercise of His grace He always acts in a way that is consistent with His other perfections. None magnified the
grace of God more than Goodwin; yet when asked, "Does
the Divine prerogative of grace mean that God saves men,
continue they what they will?" he answered,

> God forbid. We deny such a sovereignty so understood,
> as if it saved any man without rule, much less against
> rule. The very verse which speaks of God as "the God of
> all grace" in relation to our salvation adds "who hath
> called us," and our calling is a *holy* one (II Tim. 1:9).
> Though the foundation of the Lord standeth sure, yet it

is added, "Let every one that nameth the name of Christ depart from iniquity" (II Tim. 2:19), or he cannot be saved.

It helps us to gain a better understanding of this Divine title, "the God of all grace," if we compare it with another found in II Corinthians 1:3: "the God of all comfort." The main distinction between the two lies in the latter being more restricted to the dispensing aspect of God's grace, as the words that follow show: "Who comforteth us in all our tribulation" (II Cor. 1:4). As "the God of *all* comfort," He is not only the Bestower of all real consolation and the Sustainer under all trials, but also the Giver of all temporal comforts or mercies. For whatever natural refreshment or benefit we derive from His creatures is due alone to His blessing them to us. In like manner, He is the God of *all* grace: seeking grace, quickening grace, pardoning grace, cleansing grace, providing grace, recovering grace, preserving grace, glorifying grace—grace of every kind, and of full measure. Yet though the expression "the God of all comfort" serves to illustrate the title we are here considering, nevertheless, it falls short of it. For God's dispensations of grace are more extensive than those of His comfort. In certain cases God gives grace where He does not give comfort. For instance, His illuminating grace brings with it the pangs of conviction of sin, which sometimes last a lengthy season before any relief is granted. Also, under His chastening rod, sustaining grace is vouchsafed where comfort is withheld.

God Dispenses All Manner
of Grace Precisely According to Need

Not only is there every conceivable kind of grace available for us in God, but He often gives it forth precisely at the hour of our need; for then does His freely bestowed favor obtain the best opportunity in which to show itself. We are freely invited to come boldly to the throne of grace that we may "find grace to help in time of need" (Heb. 4:16), or as Solomon expressed it, that the Lord God might maintain the cause of His people Israel "at all times, as the matter shall require" (1 Kings 8:59). Such is our gracious God, ministering to us at all times as well as in all matters. The Apostle Paul declares (speaking to believers), "There hath no temptation taken you but such as is common to man [that is, but such as is ordinary to fallen human nature, for the sin against the Holy Spirit is only committed by such as have an uncommon affinity with Satan and his evil designs to thwart the gracious reign of Christ]: but God is faithful, who will not suffer you to be tempted above that ye are able; but will with the temptation also make a way of escape, that ye may be able to bear it" (I Cor. 10:13, brackets mine). The Lord Christ declared, "All manner of sin and blasphemy [with the exception just mentioned above] shall be forgiven unto men" (Matt. 12:31, brackets mine). For the God of all grace works repentance for and forgives all sorts of sins, those committed after conversion as well as those before—as the cases of David and Peter show. Says He, "I will heal their backsliding, I will love them freely" (Hos. 14:4). Full cause has each of us to say feelingly from experience, "the grace of our Lord was exceedingly abundant" (I Tim. 1:14).

The Infallible Proof of His
Abundant Grace Toward Us Who Are His

"But the God of all grace, who hath called us *unto his eternal glory*." Here is the greatest and grandest proof that

He is indeed the God of all grace to His people. No more convincing and blessed evidence is needed to make manifest the good will that he bears them. The abundant grace that is in His heart toward them and the beneficent design He has for them are made clearly evident herein. They are "the called [ones] according to his purpose" (Rom. 8:18, brackets mine), namely, that "eternal purpose which he purposed in Christ Jesus our Lord" (Eph. 3:11). The effectual call that brings forth from death to life is the first open breaking forth of God's electing grace, and it is the foundation of all the actings of His grace toward them afterwards. It is then that He commences that "good work" of His in them that He ultimately shall complete in "the day of Jesus Christ" (Phil. 1:6). By it they are called to a life of holiness here and to a life of glory hereafter. In the clause "who hath called us unto his eternal glory," we are informed that those of us who were once "by nature the children of wrath" (Eph. 2:3) but now by God's grace are "partakers of the divine nature" (II Peter 1:4) shall also be sharers of God's own eternal glory. Though God's effectual call does not bring them into the actual possession of it at once, yet it fully qualifies and fits them to partake of His glory forever. Thus the Apostle Paul tells the Colossians that he is "giving thanks unto the Father, which hath made us meet to be partakers of the inheritance of the saints in light" (Col. 1:12).

But let us look beyond the most delightful of the streams of grace to their common Fountain. It is the infinite grace that is in the nature of God that engages itself to make good His beneficent purpose and that continually supplies those streams. It is to be well noted that when God uttered that great charter of grace, "[I] will be gracious to whom I will be gracious," He prefaced it with these words: "I will make all my goodness pass before thee, and I will proclaim the name of the LORD before thee" (Exod. 33:19, brackets mine). All of that grace and mercy that is in Jehovah Himself, and that is to be made known to His people, was to engage the attention of Moses *before* his mind turned to consider the sum of His decrees or purposing grace. The veritable *ocean* of goodness that is in God is engaged in promoting the good of His people. It was that goodness that He caused to pass before His servant's eyes. Moses was heartened by beholding such an illimitable wealth of benevolence, so much so that he was fully assured that the God of all grace would indeed be gracious to those whom He had chosen in Christ before the foundation of the world. It is that *essential* grace rooted in the very being of God that is to be the first object of faith; and the more our faith is directed toward the same the more our souls will be upheld in the hour of trial, persuaded that such a One cannot fail us.

The Argument on Which Peter Bases His Petition

Fourthly, let us consider the *plea* upon which the Apostle Peter bases his request: "who hath called us unto his eternal glory by Christ Jesus." This clause is undoubtedly brought in to magnify God and to exemplify His wondrous grace. Yet considered separately, in relation to the prayer as a whole, it is the plea made by the apostle in support of the petition that follows. He was making request that God would perfect, establish, strengthen, and settle His saints. It was tantamount to arguing, "Since Thou hast already done the greater, grant them the lesser; seeing that they are to be sharers of Thine eternal glory in Christ, give them what they need while they remain in this world that is passing away." If our hearts were more engaged with *who* it is that has called us, and to *what* He has appointed us, not only would our mouths be opened wider but we should be more confident of their being filled with God's praises. It is none other than Jehovah, who sits resplendent on His throne surrounded by the adoring celestial hosts, who will shortly say to each of us, "Come unto Me and feast thyself on My perfections." Think you that He will withhold anything that is truly for your good? If He has called me to heaven, is there anything needful on earth that He will deny me?

A most powerful and prevalent plea this is! First, it is as though the apostle were saying, "Have Thou respect unto the works of Thy hand. Thou hast indeed called them out of darkness into light, but they are still fearfully ignorant. It is Thy gracious pleasure that they should spend eternity in Thine immediate presence on high, but they are here in the wilderness and are compassed with infirmities. Then, in view of both the one and the other, carry on all those other workings of grace toward and in them that are needful in order to bring them to glory." What God has already done for us should not only be a ground of confident expectation of what He shall yet do (II Cor. 1:10), but it should be used by us as an argument when making our requests to God. "Since Thou hast regenerated me, make me now to grow in grace. Since Thou hast put into my heart a hatred of sin and a hunger after righteousness, intensify the same. Since Thou hast made me a branch of the Vine, make me a very fruitful one. Since Thou hast united me to Thy dear Son, enable me to show forth His praises, to honor Him in my daily life, and thus to commend Him to those who know Him not." But I am somewhat anticipating the next division.

Our Calling and Justification a Cause for Great Praise and Expectation

In that one work of calling, God has shown Himself to be the God of all grace to you, and that should greatly strengthen and confirm your faith in Him. "Whom he called, them he also *justified*" (Rom. 8:30, ital. mine). Justification consists of two things: (1) God's forgiving us and pronouncing us to be "not guilty," just as though we had never sinned; and (2) God's pronouncing us to be righteous," just as though we had obeyed all His commandments to perfection. To estimate the plenitude of His grace in forgiveness you must calculate the number and heinousness of your sins. They were more than the hairs of your head; for you were "born like a wild ass's colt" (Job 11:12), and from the first dawnings of reason every imagination of the thoughts of your heart was only evil continually (Gen. 6:5). As for their criminality, most of your sins were committed against the voice of conscience, and they consisted of privileges despised and mercies abused. Nevertheless, His Word declares that He has "forgiven you all trespasses" (Col. 2:13). How that should melt your heart and move you to adore "the God of all grace." How it should make you fully persuaded that He will continue dealing with you not according to your deserts but according to His own goodness and benignity. True, He has not yet rid you of indwelling corruption, but that affords further occasion for Him to display His longsuffering grace toward you.

But wonderful as is such a favor, yet the forgiveness of sins is only *half* of the legal side of our salvation, and the negative and inferior part of it at that. Though everything recorded against me on the debit side has been blotted out, still there stands not a single item to my credit on the other side. From the hour of my birth to the moment of my conversion not one good deed has been registered to my account, for none of my actions proceeded from a pure principle, not being performed for God's glory. Issuing from a filthy fountain, the streams of my best works were polluted (Isa. 64:6). How then could God *justify* me, or declare me to have met the required standard? That standard is a perfect and perpetual conformity to the Divine Law, for nothing less secures its reward. Here again the wondrous riches of Divine grace appear. God has not only blotted out all my iniquities but has credited to my account a full and flawless righteousness, having imputed to me the perfect obedience of His incarnate Son. "For if by one man's offence death reigned by one; much more they which receive abundance of grace and of the *gift of righteousness* shall reign in life by one, Jesus Christ. . . . For as by one man's disobedience many were made sinners, so by the obedience of one shall many be made [that is, legally constituted] righteous" (Rom. 5:17, 19, ital. and brackets mine). When God effectually called you, He clothed you "with the robe of [Christ's] righteousness" (Isa. 61:10, brackets mine), and that investiture conveyed to you an inalienable right to the inheritance (Rom. 8:17).

Glorification Was, from the Beginning, God's Ultimate Goal for Us

"Who hath called us unto his eternal glory by Christ Jesus." When God regenerates a soul He gives him faith. By exercising faith in Christ, that which disqualified him for eternal glory (namely, his pollution, guilt, and love of sinning) is removed, and a sure title to heaven is bestowed. God's effectual call is both our qualification for, and a down payment on, eternal glory. Our glorification was the grand end that God had in view from the beginning, and all that He does for us and works in us here are but means and prerequisites to that end. Next to His own glory therein, our glorification is God's supreme design in electing and calling us. "God hath from the beginning chosen you . . . to the obtaining of *the glory* of our Lord Jesus Christ" (II Thess. 2:13, 14, ital. mine). "Moreover whom he did predestinate . . . them he also glorified" (Rom. 8:30). "Fear not, little flock; for it is your Father's good pleasure to give you the kingdom" (Luke 12:32). "Come, ye blessed of my Father, inherit the kingdom prepared for you from the foundation of the world" (Matt. 25:34). Each of these texts sets forth the fact that Christ's believing people are to inherit the heavenly kingdom and eternal glory of the triune God. Nothing less than that was what the God of all grace set His heart upon as the portion of His dear children. Hence, when our election is first made manifest by His effectual call, God is so intent upon this *glory* that He immediately gives us a title to it.

Goodwin gave a striking illustration of what we have just said from God's dealings with David. While David was but a mere shepherd boy, God sent Samuel to anoint him king in the open view of his father and brethren (I Sam. 16:13). By that solemn act God invested him with a visible and irrevocable *right* to the kingdom of Judah and Israel. His actual possession thereof God delayed for many years. Nevertheless, his Divine title thereto was bestowed at His anointing, and God engaged Himself to make it good, swearing not to repent of it. Then God suffered Saul (a figure of Satan), who marshalled all the military forces of his kingdom and most of his subjects, to do his worst. This He did in order to demonstrate that no counsel of His can be thwarted. Though for a season

David was exposed like a partridge on the mountains and had to flee from place to place, nevertheless, he was miraculously preserved by God and ultimately brought to the throne. So at regeneration God anoints us with His Spirit, sets us apart, and gives us a title to everlasting glory. And though afterwards He lets loose fierce enemies upon us, leaving us to the hardest of wrestlings and fightings with them, yet His mighty hand is over us, succoring and strengthening us and restoring us when we are temporarily overcome and taken captive.

Nothing Transitory About the Glory to Which We Are Called

God has not called us to an evanescent but to an *eternal* glory, giving us title to it at the new birth. At that time a spiritual life was communicated to the soul, a life that is indestructible, incorruptible, and therefore everlasting. Moreover, we then received "the spirit of glory" (I Peter 4:14) as "the earnest of our inheritance" (Eph. 1:13, 14). Further, the image of Christ is being progressively wrought in our hearts during this life, which the Apostle Paul calls being "changed . . . from glory to glory" (II Cor. 3:18). Not only are we thereby made 'meet to be partakers of the inheritance of the saints in light" (Col. 1:12), but we are then given an eternal *right* of glory. For by regeneration or effectual calling God begets us to the inheritance (I Peter 1:3, 4); a title thereto is given us at that moment that holds good forever. That title is ours both by the covenant stipulation of God and by the testamentary bequest of the Mediator (Heb. 9:15). "If children, then heirs; heirs of God," says Paul (Rom. 8:17). Thomas Goodwin sums it up this way:

> Put these three things together: first, that that glory we are called unto is in itself eternal; second, that that person who is called hath a degree of that glory begun in him that shall never die or perish; third, that he hath a right unto the eternity of it, and that from the time of his calling, and the argument is complete.

That "eternal glory" is "the exceeding riches of his grace" that He will lavish upon His people in the endless ages to come (Eph. 2:4-7), and as those verses tell us, even now we—legally and federally—"sit together in heavenly places in Christ Jesus."

"Who hath called us unto his eternal glory." God has not only called us into a state of grace—"this grace wherein we stand"—but to a state of glory, eternal glory, *His* eternal glory, so that we "rejoice in hope of the glory of God" (Rom. 5:2). These two things are inseparably connected: "the LORD will give grace and glory" (Ps. 84:11). Although we are the persons to be glorified by it, it is His glory that is put upon us. Obviously so, for we are wholly poor, empty creatures whom God will fill with the riches of His glory. Truly it is "the God of all grace" who does this for us. Neither creation nor providence, nor even His dealings with the elect in this life, fully displays the abundance of His grace. Only in heaven will its utmost height be seen and enjoyed. It is there that the ultimate manifestation of God's glory will be made, namely, the very honor and ineffable splendor with which Deity invests Himself. Not only shall we behold that glory forever, but it is to be communicated to us. "Then shall the righteous shine forth as the sun in the kingdom of their Father" (Matt. 13:43). The glory of God will so completely fill and irradiate our souls that it will break forth from our bodies. Then will the eternal purpose of God be fully accomplished. Then will all our fondest hopes be perfectly realized. Then will God be "all in all" (I Cor. 15:28).

Eternal Glory Is Ours by Our Union with Christ

"Who hath called us unto his eternal glory by Christ Jesus." The last part of this clause would perhaps better be translated "*in* Christ Jesus," signifying that our being called to bask in the eternal glory of God is by virtue of our union with Christ Jesus. The glory pertains to Him who is our Head, and it is communicated to us only because we are His members. Christ is the first and grand Proprietor of it, and He shares it with those whom the Father gave to Him (John 17:5, 22, 24). Christ Jesus is the Center of all the eternal counsels of God, which "he purposed in Christ Jesus our Lord" (Eph. 3:11). All the promises of God "in him [Christ] are yea, and in him Amen" (II Cor. 1:20, brackets mine). God has blessed us with all spiritual blessings in Christ (Eph. 1:3). We are heirs of God because we are joint-heirs with Christ (Rom. 8:17). As all the Divine purposes of grace were formed in Christ, so they are effectually performed and established by Him. For Zacharias, while blessing God for having "raised up an horn of salvation," added, "To perform the mercy promised to our fathers, and to remember his holy covenant" (Luke 1:68-72). We are "preserved in Jesus Christ" (Jude 1). Since God has "called [us] unto the fellowship of his Son" (I Cor. 1:9, brackets mine), that is, to be partakers (in due proportion) of all that He is partaker of Himself, Christ our Joint-heir and Representative has entered into possession of that glorious inheritance and in our names is keeping it for us (Heb. 6:20).

All Our Hope Is Bound Up in Christ Alone

Does it seem too good to be true that "the God of all grace" is *your* God? Are there times when you doubt whether He *has* personally called you? Does it surpass your faith, Christian reader, that God has actually called you to His eternal glory? Then let me leave this closing thought with you. All this is by and in *Christ Jesus*! His grace is stored up in Christ (John 1:14-18), the effectual call comes by Christ (Rom. 1:6), and the eternal glory is reached through Him. Was not *His* blood sufficient to purchase everlasting blessings for hell-deserving sinners? Then look not at your unworthiness, but at the infinite worthiness and merits of Him who is the Friend of publicans and sinners. Whether our faith takes it in or not, infallibly certain it is this prayer of His will be answered: "Father, I will that they also, whom thou hast given me, be with me where I am; that they may behold my glory" (John 17:24). That beholding will not be a transient one, such as the apostles enjoyed on the mount of transfiguration, but *for evermore*. As it has often been pointed out, when the queen of Sheba contrasted her brief visit to Solomon's court with the privilege of those who resided there, she exclaimed, "Happy are thy men, happy are these thy servants, which stand *continually* before thee" (I Kings 10:8, ital. mine). Such will be *our* blissful lot throughout the endless ages.

9

I Peter, 5:10, 11

Part 3

Having considered in the two previous chapters the supplicant, setting, Object, and plea of this prayer, let us now contemplate, fifthly, its *petition*: "the God of all grace . . . make you perfect, stablish, strengthen, settle you." The proper force of the Greek grammar would make the petition read like this: "the God of all grace . . . Himself make you perfect: Himself stablish you, Himself strengthen you, Himself settle you." There is far more contained in these words than appears on their surface. The fullness of their meaning can be discovered only by a patient searching of the Scriptures, thereby ascertaining how the several terms are used in other passages. I regard the words "Himself make you perfect" as the principal thing requested. The three words that follow are in part an amplification and in part an explanation of the process by which the desired end is reached, though each of the four words requires to be considered separately. Ancient expositors, who went into things much more deeply and thoroughly than many of our modern expositors do, raised the question as to whether this prayer receives its fulfillment in the present life or in the life to come. After carefully weighing the pros and cons of their arguments, I have concluded—taking into view the remarkable scope of the Greek word *katartizō* (no. 2675 in Strong and Thayer), here rendered *make perfect*—that this petition is granted in a twofold answer: here and hereafter. I shall therefore take in both in my comments.

Two Relevant Significations

Katartizō signifies *to make perfect* (1) by adjusting or articulating so as to produce a flawless object; or (2) by restoring an object that has become imperfect. That you may be enabled to form your own judgment, I shall set before you the passages in which the Greek word is variously translated elsewhere. In each passage quoted the word or words placed in italics is the English rendering of the Greek word translated *make perfect* in our text. When the Savior says, "a body hast thou *prepared* me [or "thou hast *fitted* me," margin]" (Heb. 10:5, ital. and brackets mine), we are to understand, as Goodwin said, that "that body was formed or articulated by the Holy Spirit, with the human soul, in all its parts, in one instant of its union with the Son of God," and that it was immaculately holy, impeccable, and without spot or blemish. *Katartizō* is used again to express the finishing and perfect consummation of God's work of the first creation: "the worlds were *framed* by the Word of God" (Heb. 11:3, ital. mine). That is to say, they were so completed that nothing more was needed for their perfection; for as Genesis 1:31 tells us, "God saw every thing that he had made, and, behold, it was very good."

But this same Greek word has a very different sense in other passages. In Matthew 4:21 it is found in the phrase "*mending* their nets," in which it denotes the repairing of what had been damaged. "Brethren, if a man be over-taken in a fault, ye which are spiritual, *restore* such an one in the spirit of meekness" (Gal. 6:1, ital. mine). In this text it signifies a restoring such as of a limb that is out of joint. No doubt this was one of the significations that the Apostle Peter had in mind when he wrote this prayer, for those for whom he prayed had been disjointed or scat-tered by persecutions (I Peter 1:1, 6, 7). Paul also had this shade of meaning before him when he exhorted the di-vided Corinthians to "*be perfectly joined together* in the same mind and in the same judgment" (I Cor. 1:10, ital. mine). Again, the word is sometimes used to express the supply of a deficiency, as it does in I Thessalonians 3:10: "that we might see your face, and *might perfect* that which is *lacking* in your faith" (ital. mine). The word *lacking* implies a deficiency. Once more, the word occurs in He-brews 13:21: "*Make* you *perfect* in every good work to do his will, working in you that which is wellpleasing in his sight." Here the apostle prays that the saints might ad-vance to further degrees of faith and holiness in this life.

Our Being Made Perfect Has to Do with the Process of Sanctification

It will thus appear, from its usage in other passages, that the Greek word rendered *make perfect* in I Peter 5:10 may yield a significance something like this: "The God of all grace . . . Himself *make* you *perfect* in all these succes-sive degrees of grace that are necessary in order for you to reach spiritual maturity." This significance does not necessarily imply any personal fault or failure in those prayed for, just as a child is not to be blamed for not having yet reached the full stature of an adult or not having attained to the knowledge that comes with mature manhood. It is with this principle in mind that God has promised to bring to perfection the good work He has begun in the souls of His people (Phil. 1:6). A Christian may walk up to the measure of grace received from above without any willful divergence in his course, and still be imperfect. This was the case with the Apostle Paul, one of the most favored of God's children, who confessed, "Not as though I had already attained, either were already perfect" (Phil. 3:12). There have been, and are, some privileged souls who never left their first love, who have followed on swiftly in pursuing the knowledge of the Lord, and who (as to the general tenor of their lives) have carried themselves according to the light received. Yet even these have needed further additions of wisdom and holiness to make them more fruitful branches of the Vine and to move them ever in the direction of a consummation of holiness in heaven.

An example of this appears in the case of the Thessalonian saints. Not only had they experienced a remarkable conversion (I Thess. 1:9), but they conducted themselves in the most God-honoring and exemplary manner so that the apostle gave thanks to God always for them on account of their "work of faith, and labour of love, and patience of hope in our Lord Jesus Christ" (vv. 2, 3). Not only were their inward graces healthy and vigorous, but in their outward conduct they were made "ensamples [patterns] to all that believe" (v. 7, brackets mine). Nevertheless, Paul was most anxious to visit them again, that he might perfect that which was lacking in their faith (I Thess. 3:10). He longed that they might be blessed with further supplies of knowledge and grace that would promote a closer walking with God and a greater resistance to and overcoming of temptations. To that faith which rests on Christ for pardon and acceptance with God, which He bestows at conversion, there is also a conscious faith that lays hold of our acceptance with God. Paul refers to this as the "full assurance of understanding" (Col. 2:2). With this blessed assurance God gives us the rich experience of "joy unspeakable and full of glory" (I Peter 1:8) and the making of our calling and election sure, so that an abundant entrance into His kingdom is begun in this life (II Peter 1:10, 11). Yet this *perfecting* also applies to the recovery and restoration of lapsed Christians, as is evident from Peter's own case.

Peter Prays for the Establishing or Confirming of Their Faith

But suppose that God should thus mend and restore those overtaken in a fault, yet might they not fall again? Yes indeed, and evidently Peter had such a contingency in view. Thus he adds the word "stablish." Peter longed that they should be so confirmed in their faith that they would not fall away. For the fickle and vacillating it was a request that they should be no more tossed to and fro, but fixed in their beliefs. For the discouraged that, having put their hands to the plow, they should not look back because of the difficulties of the way. For those who were walking closely with the Lord, that they might be established in holiness before God (I Thess. 3:13); for the most spiritual are daily in need of supporting grace. The Greek word (*stērizō* no. 4741 in Strong and Thayer) in a general way signifies *to make firm* or *confirm*. It occurs in Christ's words in Luke 16:26, "there is a great gulf *fixed*" (ital. mine). It is found again in connection with Christ and is translated, "he *stedfastly set* his face to go to Jerusalem" (Luke 9:51, ital. mine). It is the word directed by the Lord to Peter himself: "and when thou art converted, *strengthen* [or "fix firmly"] thy brethren" (Luke 22:32, ital. and brackets mine). Our Lord was commissioning Peter in advance to reestablish those of his fellow disciples who also would yield to the temptation to deny their Master. Likewise, Paul desired to establish and comfort concerning their faith the Thessalonian saints, and that in relation to temptation or trial (I Thess. 3:1-5).

Peter Prays that God Will Impart Moral Strength to Them

But though we may be so confirmed by the grace of God that we cannot totally and finally fall away, yet we are weak and may be laboring under great infirmities. Therefore the apostle adds to his petition the word "strengthen." This Greek verb (*sthenoō*, no. 4599 in Strong and Thayer) is not used elsewhere in the New Testament, but from its position here between "stablish" and settle" it appears to have the force of invigorating against weakness and corruptions. I am reminded of the prayer that Paul offered on behalf of the Ephesians, that they would be "strengthened with might by his Spirit in the inner man" (Eph. 3:16). Paul employs a negative noun (*asthenēs*, no. 772 in Strong and Thayer), formed from the same root, in Romans 5:6: "For when we were yet *without strength*, in due time Christ died for the ungodly" (ital. mine). In our unregenerate state we were entirely devoid of ability and enablement to do those things that are pleasing to God. Not only is the state of spiritual impotency of an unregenerate soul called being "*without strength*," but the state of the body when dead is expressed by a noun (*astheneia*, no. 769) derived from *asthenēs* (no. 772). "It is sown in *weakness*," that is, it is lifeless, utterly devoid of any vigor. But, by contrast, "it is raised in power" (I Cor. 15:43); that is, it is to be endued and furnished with all the abilities of rational creatures, even such as the angels have (Luke 20:36) who "excel in strength" (Ps. 103:20). Thus, this request for the strengthening of the saints is to be understood as supplies of grace that will energize weak hands and feeble knees and enable them to overcome every opposing force.

Peter Prays that They May Be Settled in Faith, Love, and Hope

Though we be confirmed so that we shall never be lost, and though we be strengthened to bear up against trials, yet we may become shaky and uncertain. Therefore Peter adds the word "settle" to his petition. He is concerned that they be unremitting in their faith in Christ, love toward God, and hope of eternal glory. The Greek verb (*themelioō*, no. 2311) is rendered *founded* in Matthew 7:25, *lay the foundation of* in Hebrews 1:10, and *grounded* in Ephesians 3:17. In our text it appears to be used as the opposite of waverings of spirit and doubtings of heart. Peter is saying something like this: "I pray that you may be able confidently to say, 'For I know whom I have believed, and am persuaded that he is able to keep that which I have committed unto him against that day' (II Tim. 1:12), and that you turn not from the path of duty because of the opposition you encounter. No matter how good the tree, if it be not settled in the earth, but moved from place to place, it will bear little or no fruit. How many might trace the unfruitfulness of their lives to the unsettled state of their hearts and judgments! David could say, "My heart is fixed, O God, my heart is fixed," and therefore he added, "I will sing and give praise" (Ps. 57:7).

This, too, is a blessing that God alone can impart. "Now to him that is of power to stablish you," says Paul (Rom. 16:25). Yet, as Deuteronomy 28:9 and II Chronicles 20:20 show, we must use the appointed means.

"Himself make you perfect: stablish, strengthen, settle you." The ultimate object seems to be mentioned first, and then the steps by which it is to be reached. But whether regarded in conjunction or singly, they all have to do with our practical sanctification. The piling up of these emphatic terms indicates the difficulty of the Christian's task and his urgent need of constant supplies of Divine grace. The saint's warfare is one of no common difficulty, and his needs are deep and many; but he has to do with "the God of all grace"! Therefore, it is both our privilege and duty to draw upon Him by importunate supplication (II Tim. 2:1; Heb. 4:16). God has provided grace answerable to our every need, yet it flows through the *means* He has appointed. God will "perfect: stablish, strengthen, settle" us in response to fervent prayer, by the instrumentality of His Word, by His blessing to us the various ministries of His servants, and by sanctifying to us the discipline of His providences. He who has given His people a sure hope will also give everything necessary to the realization of the thing hoped for (II Peter 1:3); but it is uniquely our part to seek the desired and necessary blessing by prayer (Ezek. 36:37).

Our Suffering with Christ Must
Precede Our Being Glorified with Christ

Sixthly, we come to ponder the *qualification* of this prayer: "after that ye have suffered a while." This clause is intimately connected with two others: (1) "who hath called us unto his eternal glory by Christ Jesus"; and (2) the petition "himself make you perfect. . . . " The apostle did not pray that believers be removed from this world as soon as they be regenerated, nor that they be immediately relieved of their sufferings. Rather, he prays that their sufferings should give way to eternal glory "after . . . a while," or, as the Greek signifies, "after a little while," because all time is short in comparison with eternity. For the same reason the severest afflictions are to be regarded as "light" and "but for a moment" when set over against the "eternal weight of glory" that is awaiting us (II Cor. 4:17). The sufferings and the glory are inseparably connected, for "we must through much tribulation enter into the kingdom of God" (Acts 14:22). The Apostle Paul clearly teaches that those of us who are God's children shall indeed share in Christ's inheritance, "if so be that we suffer with him, that we may be also glorified together" (Rom. 8:17). If one bear no cross, he shall gain no crown (Luke 14:27). All who have suffered for Christ's sake on earth shall be glorified in heaven; but none shall be glorified save those who, in some form or other, have been "made conformable unto his death" (Phil. 3:10). Some of the believer's sufferings are from the hand of God's providence, some from "false brethren" (II Cor. 11:26; Gal. 2:4), some from the profane world, some from Satan, and some from indwelling sin. Peter speaks of "manifold temptations" or "trials" (I Peter 1:6), but they are counterbalanced by "manifold grace" (I Peter 4:10). And both are directed by "the manifold wisdom of God" (Eph. 3:10)!

Our Conformity to Christ Necessarily Includes Our Having Fellowship with Him in His Sufferings

The abounding grace of God does not preclude trials and afflictions, but those who are the recipients of Divine grace have been "appointed thereunto" (I Thess. 3:3). Then let us not be dismayed or cast down by them, but seek grace to get them sanctified to us. Sufferings are *necessary* to the saints on various accounts. First and foremost, they are appointed in order that the members might be conformed to their Head. "For it became him, for whom are all things, and by whom are all things, in bringing many sons unto glory, to make the captain of their salvation perfect through sufferings" (Heb. 2:10). Sufficient then for the disciple to be like his Master, that he should be made perfect after he has suffered awhile. Peter himself alludes to this Divinely prescribed order in the way of salvation (namely humiliation, then exaltation, which applies not only to the Head but to His members also) when he refers to "the sufferings of Christ, and the glory that should follow" (I Peter 1:11). It was the Divine will that even the incarnate Son should "learn . . . obedience [submission] by the things which he suffered" (Heb. 5:8, brackets mine). There was a turning point in His ministry when Jesus began "to shew unto his disciples, how that he must go unto Jerusalem, and *suffer* many things of the elders and chief priests and scribes, and be killed, and be raised again the third day" (Matt. 16:21, ital. mine). Why did He have to suffer thus? It is because God had ordained it (Acts 4:28). Was Christ tempted by the devil merely on account of Satan's malice toward Him? No, for Jesus was "led up of [by] the Spirit into the wilderness to be tempted of the devil" (Matt. 4:1, brackets mine; cf. Mark 1:12, 13; Luke 4:1, 2). Remember, dear saints enduring trials, that the Savior Himself entered the kingdom of God "through much tribulation" (Acts 14:22), even as we must do. Thus, "in that he himself hath suffered being tempted, he is able to succor ["relieve" or "help"] them that are tempted" (Heb. 2:18, brackets mine). Therefore, let us "count it all joy when ye [we] fall into divers temptations" (James 1:2, brackets mine), for suffering "as a Christian" is a means by which we can glorify our redeeming God (I Peter 4:16). The privilege of experiencing "the fellowship of his sufferings" is one of God's appointed means by which we may know that we are *in Christ*, and no longer identified with the world that now abides under God's wrath (Phil. 3:7-11). Hear the words of our Master (Matt. 5:10-12):

> Blessed are they which are persecuted for righteousness' sake: for theirs is the kingdom of heaven. Blessed are ye, when men shall revile you, and persecute you, and shall say all manner of evil against you falsely, for my sake. Rejoice, and be exceeding glad: for great is your reward in heaven: for so persecuted they the prophets which were before you.

God's Grace Is Magnified in Meeting Our Needs and Confounding Our Enemies

Secondly, the God of all grace has made this appointment because His grace is best seen in sustaining us and is most manifest by relieving us. Hence, we find the throne of grace magnified by God's giving us "grace to help in time of need" (Heb. 4:16). Much of the glory of God's grace appears in His supporting the weak, in delivering the tempted, and in raising the fallen. The Lord exempts us not from conflict, but maintains us in it. Effectual calling ensures our final perseverance, yet it does not render needless continual supplies of grace. As Manton expressed it, "God will not only give them glory at the end of their journey, but bears their expenses by the way."

Thirdly, our Father leads us through fiery trials in order to confound those who are opposed to us. Grace *reigns* (Rom. 5:21), and the greatness of a monarchy is demon-

strated by its subduing of rebels and vanquishing of enemies. God raised up the mighty Pharaoh in order to show
forth His own power. In the context (I Peter 5:8), as we
have seen, He suffers the devil, as a roaring lion, to rage
up and down opposing and assaulting us. But He does
this only to foil him, for "the prey [shall] be taken from
the mighty" (Isa. 49:24, brackets mine), and shortly God
shall "bruise Satan under your [our] feet" (Rom. 16:20,
brackets mine).

Suffering Proves Our Graces and Makes Heaven More Glorious

Fourthly, suffering is necessary for the trying and prov-
ing of our graces: "the trying of your faith worketh patience" (James 1:3). Consider what Peter says concerning
us who have been "begotten . . . again unto a lively hope":

> Wherein ye greatly rejoice, though now for a season, if
> need be, ye are in heaviness through manifold tempta-
> tions: That the trial of your faith, being much more pre-
> cious than of gold that perisheth, though it be tried with
> fire, might be found unto praise and honour and glory at
> the appearing of Jesus Christ (I Peter 1:6, 7).

It is the wind of tribulation that separates the wheat from
the chaff, the furnace that reveals the difference between
dross and gold. The stony-ground hearer is offended and
falls away "when tribulation or persecution ariseth because of the word" (Matt. 13:21). So, too, for the purifying
and the brightening of our hope, our hearts have to be
more completely weaned from this world before they become *set* upon things above.

Fifthly, the glory of our eternal inheritance is enhanced

by our enduring affliction. Hear the words of Thomas Goodwin:

> Heaven is not simply joy and happiness, but a glory, and a glory *won by conquest*—"to him that overcometh" [are the promises made] in each one of the seven epistles of Revelation 2 and 3. It is a crown won by mastery, and so by striving, according to certain laws set to be observed by those that win (II Tim. 2:5). The glory won by conquest and masteries is the more valuable. The portion Jacob won "with my sword and with my bow" was the one he reserved for his beloved Joseph (Gen. 48:22). We are more than conquerors through Him that loved us.

Grace Is Provided for Both Internal and External Conflicts

It is a mistake (made by some) to restrict either the afflictions of verse 9 or the suffering of verse 10 to *outward* persecutions and trials. But all *inward* assaults (whether from our own lusts or Satan), and so all temptations whatsoever, are to be included. The context requires this, for the words "be sober, be vigilant" have respect to our lusts as well as to every other provocation to evildoing, so that the call to resist the devil clearly relates to his inward temptations to sin. The experience of all saints requires it, for their acutest pangs are occasioned by their own corruptions. Moreover, as Goodwin has pointed out, our setting of God before the eyes of our faith as "the God of all grace" argues the same; for His grace stands principally ready to help us against inward sins and temptations to sin. Furthermore, the *all* of His grace extends not only to all sorts of external miseries, but to all *internal* maladies, which are our greatest grief, which require His abundant grace above all others, and to which His grace is chiefly directed (Ps. 19:14; 119:1-16; Prov. 3:5-7; 4:20-27). His grace is the grand remedy for every evil to which the believer is subject. Some are guilty of worse sins after conversion than before, and were not the God of *all* grace their God, where would they be?

Perfection in Grace Is Both Progressive and Eschatological

"After that ye have suffered a while, Himself make you perfect: stablish, strengthen, settle you." This may well be regarded as a request for grace to enable us to obey the exhortation found in I Corinthians 15:58: "Therefore, my beloved brethren, be ye stedfast, unmoveable, always abounding in the work of the Lord." We are to be constantly opposing sin and striving to be holy in all manner of conversation. This request receives a partial fulfillment in this life, but a complete and more transcendent one in heaven. Saints are advanced to further degrees of faith and holiness when, after seasons of wavering and suffering, God strengthens and establishes them in a more settled frame of spirit. Yet only in our fixed condition after death will these blessings be fully ours. Not till then shall we be *made perfect* in the sense of being fully conformed to the image of God's Son. Our hearts will be established "unblameable in holiness before God, even our Father, at the coming of our Lord Jesus Christ" (I Thess. 3:13). Only then will all our weakness end and our bodies be "raised in power" (I Cor. 15:43). Then indeed shall we be eternally settled, for the Divine promise is this: "Him that overcometh will I make a pillar in the temple of my God, and he shall go no more out" (Rev. 3:12).

A Doxology of Infallible Hope

Seventh and finally, we come to the great *ascription* of this apostolic prayer: "to him be glory and dominion for ever and ever. Amen." "The apostle, having added prayer to his doctrine, here added praise to his prayer," says Leighton. It expressed the apostle's confidence that the God of all grace would grant his request. He was assured that what he had asked for on behalf of the saints would be to the Divine "glory," and that the Divine "dominion" would infallibly bring it to pass. There is thus a practical hint implied for us in this closing doxology. It intimates *where* relief is to be obtained and strength is to be found in the midst of our suffering: by eyeing the glory of God, which is the grand end He has in view in all His dealings with us; and by confidently trusting in God's dominion in working all things together for our good (Rom. 8:28). For if *His* be the dominion, and He has called us to His eternal glory, then what have we to fear? So certain is our glorification (Rom. 8:30) that we should give thanks for it now. The abundant and infinite grace of God is engaged to effect it, and His omnipotent power guarantees its performance.

10
II Peter 1:2, 3

No thorough study of the prayers of the apostles, or of the prayers of the Bible as a whole, would be complete without an examination of the benedictions with which the apostles (James excepted), prefaced their Epistles. Those opening salutations were very different from a mere act of politeness, as when the chief captain of the Roman soldiers at Jerusalem wrote a letter after this manner: "Claudius Lysias unto the most excellent governor Felix sendeth greeting" (Acts 23:26). Far more than a courteous formality were their introductory addresses, yea, even than the expressions of a kindly wish. Their "grace be unto you and peace" was a *prayer*, an act of worship, in which Christ was always addressed in union with the Father. It signifies that a request for these blessings had been made before the throne. Such benedictions evinced the warm affection in which the apostles held those to whom they wrote, and breathed forth their spiritual desires on their behalf. By putting these words of blessing at the very beginning of his Epistle, the Apostle

Peter made manifest how powerfully his own heart was affected by the goodness of God toward his brethren.

That which is now to engage our attention may be considered under the following heads. First we shall look at the *substance* of the prayer: "grace and peace"—these are the blessings besought of God. Secondly, we shall ponder the desired *measure* of their bestowal: "be multiplied unto you." Thirdly, we shall contemplate the *medium* of their conveyance: "through the knowledge of God, and of Jesus our Lord." Fourthly, we shall *examine* the motive prompting the request: "According as his Divine power hath given unto us all things that pertain unto life and godliness" (v. 3). Before filling in that outline or giving an exposition of those verses, let us point out (especially for the benefit of young preachers, for whom it is especially vital to learn *how* a text should be pondered) what is *implied* by this prayer.

The Vital Implications of This Benediction

In the apostle's seeking from God such blessings as these for the saints the following vital lessons are taught by implication: (1) that none can merit anything at the hands of God, for grace and merit are opposites; (2) that there can be no real peace apart from Divine grace—"There is no peace, saith my God, to the wicked" (Isa. 57:21); (3) that even the regenerate stand in need, constant need, of grace from God; and (4) the regenerate, therefore, should be vile in their own eyes. If we would receive more from God, then we must present our hearts to Him as empty vessels. When Abraham was about to make request of the Lord, he demeaned himself as "dust and ashes" (Gen. 18:27); and Jacob acknowledged that he was not worthy of the least of His mercies (Gen. 32:10). (5) Such a request as Peter is here making is a tacit confession of the utter dependence of believers upon God's bounty, that He alone is able to supply their need. (6) In asking for grace and peace to be *multiplied* to them, acknowledgment is made that not only the beginning and continuance of them, but also their increase proceeds from the good pleasure of God. (7) Intimation is hereby given that we may "open thy [our] mouth wide" (Ps. 81:10, brackets mine) to God. Yea, it is an ill sign to be contented with a little grace. "He was never good that doth not desire to grow better," says Manton.

The Special Character of the Second Epistles

A word needs also to be said upon the character of the book in which this particular prayer is found. Like all *second* Epistles, this one treats of a state of affairs where false teaching and apostasy had a more or less prominent place. One of the principal differences between his two Epistles is this: whereas in his first Epistle Peter's main design was to strengthen and comfort his brethren amid the suffering to which they were exposed from the profane (heathen) world (see chapter 4), and he now graciously warns (II Peter 2:1; 3:1-4) and confirms (II Peter 1:5-11; 3:14) them against a worse peril from the professing world, from those *within* Christendom who menaced them. In his first Epistle Peter had represented their great adversary, the devil, as a roaring lion (I Peter 5:8). But here, without directly naming him, he depicts Satan as an angel of light (but in reality the subtle serpent), who is no longer persecuting, but seeking to corrupt and poison them through false teaching. In the second chapter those false teachers are denounced (1) as men who had denied the Lord that bought them (v. 1), and (2) as licentious (vv. 10-14, 19), giving free play to their carnal appetites.

The Apostle Peter addresses his Epistle "to them that have obtained like precious faith with us through the righteousness of our God and our Saviour Jesus Christ" (II Peter 1:1; word order here is according to the Greek text and KJV marginal note). The word *faith* here refers to that act of the soul whereby Divinely revealed truth is savingly apprehended. Their faith is declared to be "precious," for it is one of God's choicest gifts and the immediate fruit of His Spirit's regenerating power. This is emphasized in the expression "have obtained" (*lagchanō*, no. 2975 in Strong and Thayer). It is the same Greek word found in Luke 1:9: "his *lot was* to burn incense" (ital. mine). It appears again in John 19:14: "Let us not rend it, but *cast lots* for it" (ital. mine). Thus these saints were reminded that they owed their saving faith not to any superior sagacity of theirs, but solely to the allotments of grace. It had been with them as with Peter himself. A *revelation* had been made to them: not by flesh and blood, but by the heavenly Father (Matt. 16:17). In the dispensing of God's favors a blessed portion had fallen to them, even "the faith of God's elect" (Titus 1:1). The *them* whom Peter addresses are the Gentiles, and the *us* in which he includes himself are the Jews. Their faith had for its *object* the perfect righteousness of Christ their Surety, for the words "through the righteousness of" are probably better translated and understood "*in* the righteousness of" the Divine Savior.

The Substance of Peter's Benediction

Having thus described his readers by their spiritual standing, Peter adds his apostolic benediction: "*grace and peace* be multiplied unto you." The combined apostolic benediction and greeting (which contains the elements *grace* and *peace*) is essentially the same as that employed by Paul in ten of his Epistles as well as by Peter in I Peter. In I and II Timothy and Titus, Paul added the element *mercy*, as did John in II John. Jude used the elements *mercy*, *peace*, and *love*. Thus we learn that the apostles, in pronouncing Spirit-indited blessings upon the believers to whom they wrote, combined *grace*, the watchword of the New Covenant age (John 1:14, 17) with *peace*, the distinctive Hebrew blessing. Those who have read the Old Testament attentively will remember how frequently the salutation "peace be unto thee" or something similar is found (Gen. 43:23; Judg. 6:23; 18:6; etc.). "Peace be within thy walls, and prosperity within thy palaces" (Ps. 122:7), cries David, as he expectantly contemplates the spiritual and temporal blessings that he desires for Jerusalem and thus for Israel (cf. vv. 6, 8, as well as the whole Psalm). This text shows that the word *peace* was a general term to denote *welfare*. From its use by the risen Savior in John 20:19, we gather that it was an all-inclusive summary of blessing. In the Epistles and the Book of Revelation (which was meant by Christ, the great Head of the Church, to circulate after the fashion of an Epistle), the terms *grace* and/or *peace* are frequently used in closing salutations and benedictions. The word *peace* is used in various ways eight times (Rom. 16:20; II Cor. 13:11; Eph. 6:23; I Thess. 5:23; II Thess. 3:16; Heb. 13:20; I Peter 5:14; III John 14), six of those times in greater or lesser proximity to the word *grace*, which is used eighteen times (Rom. 16:20, 24; I Cor. 16:23; II Cor. 13:14; Gal. 6:18; Eph. 6:24; Phil. 4:23; Col. 4:18; I Thess. 5:28; II Thess. 3:18; I Tim. 6:21; II Tim. 4:22; Titus 3:15; Philem. 24; Heb. 13:25; I Peter 5:10; II Peter 3:18; Rev. 22:21). Obviously, the clause "The grace of our Lord Jesus Christ be with you," or some variation upon it, is the most characteristic benedictory close employed by the apostles. In light of his grasp of the glorious realities of the Gospel age (Acts 10, 11, especially vv. 1-18), it is evident by this benediction that the Apostle Peter sees and embraces both believing Jews and believing Gentiles as united in sharing the full blessing of God's great salvation.

Having an earnest desire for their welfare, Peter sought for the saints the choicest bounties that could be conferred upon them, that they might be morally and spiritually enriched, both inwardly and outwardly. "Grace and peace" contain the sum of Gospel bestowals and the supply of our every need. Together they include all manner of blessings, and therefore they are the most comprehensive things that can be requested of God. They are the choicest favors we can desire for ourselves, *and for our brethren*! They are to be sought by faith from God our Father in reliance upon the mediation and merits of our Lord Jesus Christ. "Grace and peace" are the very essence, as well as the whole, of a believer's true happiness in this life, which explains the apostle's longing that his brethren in Christ might abundantly partake of them.

Peter Prays for Growth in Grace in His Brethren

Grace is not to be understood in the sense of God's distinguishing, redeeming favor, for these saints were already the objects thereof; nor is it to be taken as an inward spiritual principle of nature, for that was imparted to them at the new birth. Rather, it refers to a greater manifestation of the spiritual nature and Divine likeness that one has received from God and a greater and more cheerful dependence upon the Giver (II Cor. 12:9). It also refers to the Divine gifts that induce such growth. Speaking of Christ, the Apostle John declares, "And of his fulness have all we received, and grace for ["upon," ASV margin] grace" (John 1:16, brackets mine). Matthew Poole comments as follows:

> *And grace for grace*: nor have we received drops, but grace *upon* grace; not only knowledge and instruction, but the love and favour of God, and spiritual habits, in proportion to the favour and grace which Christ hath (allowing for our short capacities); we have received grace freely and plentifully, all from Christ, and for His sake; which lets us see how much the grace-receiving soul is bound to acknowledge and adore Christ, and may be confirmed in the receiving of *further* grace, and the hopes of eternal life . . . (italics mine).

It is evident from I Peter 4:10 that God's grace is *manifold*, being dispensed to His saints in various forms and amounts according to their needs, yet for the edification not only of the individual but of the Body of Christ as a whole (Eph. 4:7-16). At the very end of this Epistle Peter commands his readers, saying, "But grow in grace, and in the knowledge of our Lord and Savior Jesus Christ" (II Peter 3:18; cf. Eph. 4:15). Thus we see the propriety of Peter's prayer, that God would further exercise His benignity toward them. We also see the necessity of our praying in the same way for ourselves and for each other.

Thus we see that though the fundamental meaning and reference of *grace* is to the freely bestowed, redeeming favor of God, yet the term is often used in a wider sense to include all those blessings that flow from His sovereign kindness. In this way is it to be so understood in the apostolic benedictions: a prayer for the continued and increased expression and manifestation of the good work that He has already begun (Phil. 1:6). "Grace and peace." The two benefits are fitly joined together, for the one is never found without the other. Without reconciling grace there can be no solid and durable peace. The former is God's good will *toward* us; the latter is His grand work *in* us. In the proportion that grace is communicated, peace is enjoyed: grace to sanctify the heart; peace to comfort the soul.

Though Peace Begins with Justification, It Is Maintained by Our Obedience

Peace is one of the principal fruits of the Gospel as it is received into a believing heart, being that tranquility of mind that arises from the sense of our acceptance with God. It is not an objective but a subjective peace that is here in view. "Peace *with* God" (Rom. 5:1, ital. mine) is fundamentally *judicial*, being what Christ made for His people (Col. 1:20). Yet faith conveys a response to the conscience concerning our amity with God. In the proportion that our faith rests upon the peace made with God by the blood of Christ, and of our acceptance in Him, will be our inward peace. In and through Christ, God is at peace with believers, and the happy effect of this in our hearts is a felt "righteousness, and peace, and joy in the Holy Ghost" (Rom. 14:17). But we are not in a capacity to receive and enjoy those blessings until we have surrendered to Christ's Lordship and taken His yoke upon us (Matt. 11:29, 30). It is appropriate, therefore, for Paul to say, "And let the peace of God *rule* in your hearts" (Col. 3:15, ital. mine). *This* is the kind of peace that the apostles prayed for on behalf of their brethren. This peace is the fruit of a Scriptural assurance of God's favor, which, in turn, comes from the maintenance of communion with Him by an obedient walk. It is also peace with *ourselves*. We are at peace with ourselves when conscience ceases to accuse us, and when

our affections and wills submit themselves to an enlightened mind. Furthermore, it includes concord and amity
with our fellow Christians (Rom. 5:5, 6). What an excellent example was left us by the church in Jerusalem: "And
the multitude of them that believed were of *one heart* and
of one soul" (Acts 4:32, ital. mine).

The Measure of Bestowal Desired: A Multiplication of Grace and Peace

Grace and peace are the present heritage of God's
people, and of them Peter desired that they should enjoy
much, much more than a mere sip or taste. As I Peter 3:18
intimates, he longed that they should "grow in grace,"
and that they might be filled with peace (cf. Rom 15:13);
he thus made request accordingly. "Grace and peace be
multiplied unto you." By these words Peter calls upon God
to visit them with still larger and more lavish displays of
His goodness. He prays not only that God might grant to
them greater and greater manifestations of His grace and
peace, but also that their feeble capacities to apprehend
what God had done for their souls might be greatly enlarged. He prays that an abundant supply of grace and
peace should be conferred upon them. They were already
the favored partakers of those Divine benefits, but request
was made for a plentiful increase of them. Spiritual things
(unlike material) do not cloy in the enjoyment of them,
and therefore we cannot have too much of them. The
words "peace be multiplied" intimate that there are degrees of assurance concerning our standing with God, and
that we never cease to be dependent upon free grace. The
dimensions of this request teach us that it is our privilege
to ask God not only for more grace and peace, but for an
amplitude thereof. God is most honored when we make

the largest demands upon His bounty. If our spirits are straitened in their enjoyment of God's grace and peace, it is due to the paltriness of our prayers and never to any niggardliness in Him.

The Medium by Which Grace and Peace Are Conveyed

"Through the knowledge of God, and of Jesus our Lord." The careful reader, who is not too dilatory in comparing Scripture with Scripture, will have observed a variation from the salutation used by Peter in his first Epistle (I Peter 1:2). There he prayed, "Grace unto you, and peace, be multiplied." The addition ("through the knowledge of God," etc.) made here is a significant one, in keeping with Peter's altered design and appropriate to his present aim. The student may also have noted that *knowledge* is one of the prominent words of this Epistle (see II Peter 1:2, 3, 5, 6, 8; 2:20; 3:18). We should also consider how frequently the Christ is designated *"our* Lord" or *"our* Saviour" (II Peter 1:1, 2, 8, 11, 14, 16; 3:15, 18), by which Peter draws a sharp contrast between true disciples and those false professors of Christianity who will not submit to Christ's scepter. That "knowledge of God" alluded to here is not a natural but a spiritual knowledge, not speculative, but experiential. Nor is it merely a knowledge of the God of creation and providence, but of a God who is in covenant with men through Jesus the Christ. This is evident from its being mentioned in connection with the words "and of Jesus our Lord." It is therefore an evangelical knowledge of God that is here in view. He cannot be savingly known except in and through Christ even as Christ Himself declared: "neither knoweth any man the Father, save the Son, and he to whomsoever the Son will reveal him" (Matt. 11:27).

Inasmuch as this prayer was for grace and peace to be "multiplied" to the saints "through [or *in*] the knowledge of God," there was a tacit intimation that they would both abide and advance in that knowledge. Calvin comments as follows:

> *Through the knowledge*, literally, *in the knowledge*; but the preposition *en* [no. 1722 in Strong and Thayer] often means "through" or "with": yet both senses may suit the context. I am, however, more disposed to adopt the former. For the more any one advances *in* the knowledge of God, every kind of blessing increases also equally with the sense of Divine love.

A spiritual and experiential knowledge of God is the grand *means* by which all the influences of grace and peace are conveyed to us. God works upon us as *rational* creatures in a way that is agreeable to our intellectual and moral nature, with knowledge preceding all else. As there is no real peace apart from grace, so there is no grace or peace without a saving knowledge of God; and no such knowledge of Him is possible but *in* and *through* "Jesus our Lord," for Christ is the channel by which every blessing is transmitted to the members of His mystical Body. As the more windows a house has the more sunlight enters it, so the greater our knowledge of God the greater our measure of grace and peace. But the evangelical knowledge of the most mature saint is only fragmentary and feeble, and thus requires continual augmentation by the Divine blessing upon those means that have been appointed for its perfecting and strengthening.

The Divine Accomplishment that Moved Peter to Prayer

"According as his divine power hath given unto us all things that pertain unto life and godliness, through the

knowledge of him that hath called us to glory and virtue"
(v. 3). Therein the apostle found his *motive* for making the
above request. It was because God had *already* wrought
so wondrously on behalf of these saints that he was moved
to ask Him to continue dealing lavishly with them. We
may also regard this third verse as being brought in to
encourage *the faith* of these Christians: that, since God
had done such great things for them, they should expect
further liberal supplies from Him. Notice that the inspiring motive was a purely evangelical one, and not legal or
mercenary. God had bestowed upon them everything
needful for the production and preservation of spirituality
in their souls, and the apostle longed to see them maintained in a healthy and vigorous condition. Divine power
is the foundation of spiritual life, grace is what supports
it, and peace is the atmosphere in which it thrives. The
words "all things that pertain unto life and godliness"
may also be understood as referring ultimately to eternal
life in glory: a right to it, a fitness for it, and an earnest
of it had already been bestowed upon them.

Finally, it is essential to our Christian growth to realize
that the contents of verse 3 are to be regarded as the
ground of the exhortation in verses 5 through 7. Thus the
supply asked for in verse 2 is to be regarded as the necessary *equipment* for all spiritual fruit bearing and good
works. Let us then exercise the greater diligence to abide
in Christ (John 15:1-5) both in our prayers and in all our
thoughts, words, and deeds.

11

Jude 24, 25

Part 1

The prayer that is now to engage our attention is a particularly arresting one, but its beauty and blessedness appear even more conspicuously when it is examined in connection with its somber *background*. It concludes the most solemn Epistle in the New Testament, one that is to be read with fear and trembling, but that is to be put down with thanksgiving and praise. It contains a most awful description of graceless professors of Christianity, of those trees who appeared to give much promise of fruit to God's glory but whose leaves soon dropped off and who quickly withered away. Its theme is apostasy, or, more specifically, the corrupting of much of the visible Church and the resulting ongoing corruption of an apostate Christendom. It presents a picture that all too tragically depicts things as they now are in the religious realm, in the majority of so-called "churches" at large. It informs us as to how the process of declension begins in reprobate professors of religion and how it works itself out until they are completely corrupted. It delineates the characters of those who lead others astray in this vile work. It makes known the sure doom awaiting both leaders and those who are led into apostasy. It closes with a glorious contrast.

Many Pervert the Gospel of Free Grace into a License to Sin

The Lord Jesus gave warning that the sowing of the good seed by Himself and His apostles would be followed with the sowing of tares in the same field by Satan and his agents. Paul also announced that, notwithstanding the widespread successes of the Gospel during his lifetime, there would be "a falling away" before the man of sin should be revealed (II Thess. 2:3). That "falling away," or the apostasy of the visible Church corporately considered, is depicted by the Spirit in some detail through the pen of Jude. As Christ Himself had intimated, the initial work of corruption would be done stealthily, "while men slept" (Matt. 13:25), and Jude represents the evildoers as having "crept in unawares" (v. 4), that is, having slipped in secretly or surreptitiously. They are spoken of as men who were "turning the grace of our God into lasciviousness, and denying the only Lord God, and our Lord Jesus Christ." That is to say, while pretending to *magnify* free grace they *perverted* it, failing to enforce the balancing truth of holiness; and while professing to believe in Christ as a *Savior* they refused to surrender to His *Lordship*. Thus they were lustful and lawless. In view of this horrible menace, the saints were exhorted to "earnestly contend for the faith which was once delivered unto the saints" (v. 3). In this context, *faith* signifies nothing less than the whole counsel of God (cf. Acts 20:27-31).

That exhortation is enforced by a reminder to three fearful and solemn examples of the punishment visited by God upon those who had apostatized. The first is that of the children of Israel whom the Lord saved out of Egypt, but who still lusted after its fleshpots; and because of their unbelief at Kadesh-Barnea a whole generation of them were destroyed in the wilderness (v. 5; cf. Num. 13;14:1-39, especially vv. 26-37). The second is the case of those angels who had apostatized from their privileged position, and are now "reserved in everlasting chains under darkness unto the judgment of the great day" (v. 6). The third is Sodom and Gomorrah, which, because of their common indulgence in the grossest form of lasciviousness, were destroyed by fire from heaven (v. 7; cf. Gen. 19:1-25). To which the apostle adds that the corruptors of the visible Church "defile the flesh, despise dominion, and speak evil of dignities," being less respectful to their superiors than Michael the archangel was to his inferior (vv. 8, 9). He solemnly pronounces the Divine sentence: "Woe unto them!" (v. 11). Without the slightest hesitation, he likens them and their works to three characters of evil notoriety: by "the way of Cain" we are to understand a flesh-gratifying, natural religion that is acceptable to the unregenerate; by "the error of Balaam for reward" a mercenary ministry that will pervert the pure "doctrine of true religion for the sake of filthy lucre" (Calvin); and by "the gainsaying of Korah" a despising of authority and discipline, an effort to obliterate the distinctions that God has made for His own glory and for our good (Num. 16:1-3).

Jude Gives Clear Indication that These Falsifiers Are Within the Churches

Other characteristics of these religious evildoers are given in figurative terms in verses 12 and 13. It should be particularly noted that they are said to "feast *with you*" (the saints), which supplies further evidence that such hypocrites, deceivers and self-deceived, are *inside* the churches. In the second half of verse 13 through verse 15 their doom is pronounced. For backsliders there is a way of recovery; but for apostates there is none. In verse 16 Jude details other characteristics of false brethren, which traits are sadly conspicuous in many professing Christians of our own day. Then Jude bids God's people to remember that the apostles of Christ had predicted there should be "mockers [or "scoffers," no. 1703 in Strong and Thayer (II Peter 3:3)] in the last time, who should walk after their own ungodly lusts" (vv. 17, 18). By "the last time" is meant this Christian or final dispensation (see I Peter 4:7; I John 2:18), with a possible reference to the climactic culmination of evil at its end. Next, Jude appeals to those to whom he is writing, addressing to them a number of needful and salutary exhortations (vv. 21-23). He ends with the prayer that we are now to ponder, concluding the most solemn of all the Epistles with a more glorious outburst of praise than is elsewhere to be found in them.

Jude's Concluding Paean to the Triumphant Grace of God

"Now unto him that is able to keep you from falling, and to present you faultless before the presence of his glory with exceeding joy, To the only wise God our Saviour, be glory and majesty, dominion and power, both now and ever. Amen." Let us consider four things in our study of this prayer: (1) its general *background*; (2) its more immediate *connection*; (3) the *reasons* that moved Jude to pray thus; and (4) the *nature and Object* of this prayer.

First, let me add something more to what has already been said, in a general way, upon the *background* of this prayer. It seems to me that, in view of what had been engaging the mind of the apostle in the previous verses, he could not restrain himself from giving vent to this paean of praise. After viewing the solemn case of a whole generation of Israel perishing in the wilderness because of their unbelief, he was moved to cry out in gladness, "Now unto him that is able to keep *you* from falling." As he contemplated the experience of the sinless angels who fell from their first estate, he could not but tremble; but when he thought of the Savior and Protector of His Church, he burst forth into a strain of adoration. Jude found great comfort and assurance in the blessed fact that the One who begins a work of grace within those given to Him by the Father will never cease from it until He has perfected it (Phil. 1:6). He knew that were it not for everlasting love and infinite power, *our* case would yet be the same as that of the angels who fell, that but for an almighty Redeemer we too must enter everlasting darkness and endure the suffering of eternal fire. Realizing that, Jude could not but bless the One whose protecting hand covers each of those purchased by His blood.

Jude Balances a Fearful Consideration of Apostasies with Confident Praise to a Preserving God

After making mention of those fearful examples of falling, it is highly probable that the thoughts of the penman of this Epistle turned to another one much more recent, and which had come beneath his own immediate notice. It is quite possible that, when our Lord sent forth the twelve, "Judas [Jude] the brother of James, and Judas Iscariot" were paired together (Luke 6:16, brackets mine; 9:1-6)—the great apostate "son of perdition" (John 17:12) and the one who was to write at length upon the great apostasy! It scarcely admits of doubt that as Jude's mind reverted to the traitor it made him exclaim with added emphasis, "Now unto him that is able to keep you from falling . . . be glory . . . both now and ever." He had probably respected Judas Iscariot as his fellow apostles had, and perhaps had heard him ask along with the others, "Lord, is it I?" in response to Christ's statement that one of their number was about to betray Him. And no doubt he was shocked when Judas Iscariot began to openly reveal his true character. For immediately after receiving the sop that Jesus had dipped in the dish for him and hearing a *woe* pronounced upon himself, Judas hypocritically repeated the question, "Master, is it I?" then went forth to do that most despicable deed for which he had been appointed (John 6:70; Matt. 26:20-25; John 13:21-30; Ps. 41:9; John 17:12). He could not but be aware that in remorse the traitor had hanged himself: and I believe that the shadow of his awful doom fell upon Jude as he penned this Epistle.

But Jude did not suffer these sad contemplations to sink him into a state of dejection. He knew that his omniscient Master had foretold that a rising tide of evil would spread through the visible Church, and that however mysterious such a phenomenon might be there was a wise reason for it in the Divine economy. He knew that however fiercely the storm might rage there was no occasion to fear, for Christ Himself was in the ship who had declared, "and, lo, I am with you alway, even unto the end of the world [or "age"]" (Matt. 28:20, brackets mine). He knew that the gates of hell could not and would not prevail against the Church (Matt. 16:18). Therefore he lifted up his eyes above this present evil age and gazed by faith upon the enthroned Head and Preserver of the Church, rendering worship to Him. *That* is the all-important lesson to be drawn from the background of this prayer, and why I have dwelt so long upon it. Fellow Christians, let us duly *heed* it. Instead of being so much occupied with conditions in the world, with the menace of the atomic bomb, with the deepening apostasy, let our hearts be increasingly engaged with our beloved Lord; let us find our peace and joy in Him.

God's Promise to Keep Us from Falling Is Connected to Our Duty to Keep Ourselves

Let us now consider the more immediate *connection* of this prayer. On former occasions we have seen how helpful it was to attend closely to the context. It is necessary to do so here if the balance of truth is to be maintained and a proneness to antinomianism is to be checked. It is not honest to lay hold of the promise implied in this prayer, "Now unto him that is able to keep you from falling," unless we have first given heed to the commandment of verse 21: "*Keep yourselves* in the love of God, . . . " (ital. mine). The precepts and promises may be distinguished, yet they are not to be separated. The former make known our duty, while the latter are for our encouragement as long as we genuinely and earnestly seek to perform the same. But one who neglects his duty is entitled to no comfort. After describing at length the beginning, the course, and the end of the apostasy of the visible Church, the apostle adds seven brief exhortations to the saints in verses 20-23. These call for the exercise of faith, prayer, love, hope, compassion, fear, and godly hatred. These exhortations are *means* to preserve us from apostasy. Calvin began his comments on these exhortations by saying this:

He shows the manner in which they could overcome all the devices of Satan, that is, by having love connected with faith, and by standing on their guard as it were in their watch-tower, until the coming of Christ.

The Proper Use of Precepts, Warnings, and Comforting Doctrines

Let us give reverent attention to the faithful words of Adolph Saphir on this life-or-death subject:

There is a one-sided and unscriptural forgetfulness of the actual position of the believer (or professing believer) as a man who is still on the road, in the battle; who has still the responsibility of trading with the talent entrusted, of watching for the return of the Master. Now there are many bypaths, dangers, precipices on the road, and we must persevere to the end. Only they who overcome and are faithful to death shall be crowned. It is not spiritual but carnal to take the blessed and solemn doctrines of our election in Christ and of the perseverance of the saints, given us as a cordial for fainting hours and as the inmost and ultimate secret of the soul in its dealings with God, and place them on the common and daily road of our duties and trials, *instead* of the precepts and warnings of the Divine Word. It is not merely that God keeps us through these warnings and commandments, but the attitude of soul which neglects and hurries over these portions of Scripture is not childlike, humble, and sincere. The attempts to explain away the fearful warnings of Scripture against apostasy are rooted in a very morbid and dangerous state of mind. A precipice is a precipice, and it is folly to deny it. "If we live after the flesh," says the apostle, "we shall die." Now, to keep people from falling over a precipice, we do not put up a slender and graceful hedge of flowers, but the strongest barrier we can; and piercing spikes or cutting pieces of glass to prevent calamities. But even this is only the surface of the matter. Our walk with God and our perseverance to the end are great and solemn realities. We are dealing with the living God, and only life with God, and in God, and unto God, can be of any avail here. He who brought us out of Egypt is now guiding us; and if we follow Him, and follow Him to the end, we shall enter into the final rest.

It is outside my intended scope to give here a full exposition of the precepts found in verses 20-23, yet a few remarks are needed if I am to be faithful in observing the inseparable link that exists between them and our text. Duty and privilege must not be divorced, nor dare we allow privilege to oust duty. If it be the Christian's privilege to have his heart engaged with Christ in glory, it must be while treading the path that He has appointed and while engaged in those tasks that He has assigned him. Though Christ is most certainly the One who keeps him from making shipwreck of the faith, it is not apart from the disciple's own earnest endeavors that He does so. Christ deals with His redeemed as reponsible creatures. He requires them to conduct themselves as moral agents, putting forth every effort to overcome the evils that menace them. Though entirely dependent on Him, they are not to remain passive. Man is of an active nature, and therefore must grow either better or worse. Before regeneration he is indeed spiritually dead, but at the new birth he receives Divine life. Motion and exercise follow life, and those motions are to be *directed* by the Divine precepts. Hear the words of our Lord:

> He that hath my commandments, and keepeth them, he it is that loveth me: and he that loveth me shall be loved of my Father, and I will love him, and will manifest myself to him.

How these words must have reechoed in Jude's memory as he wrote this Epistle (see John 14:21, 22).

Seven Exhortations to a Life of Holiness

"But ye, beloved [in contrast with the apostates of the previous verse], building up yourselves on your most holy faith" (v. 20, brackets mine). Truly, as Paul says, "the foundation of God standeth sure, having this seal, The Lord knoweth them that are his" (II Tim. 2:19a). Yet God requires that we wholeheartedly concur with Him, by our own endeavors, in *His purpose* for electing such as we to eternal salvation, namely, our entire sanctification (I Thess. 4:3). For in the same verse Paul declares, "Let every one that nameth the name of Christ depart from iniquity" (I Tim. 2:19b). Therefore, we are to be solicitous about our growth and to exercise care both over ourselves and our fellow believers. It is not sufficient to be grounded in the faith; we must daily increase therein more and more. To grow in faith is one of the appointed *means* of our preservation. We build up ourselves on our faith by a deepened knowledge thereof. "A wise man will hear, and will increase learning"; says Solomon (Prov. 1:5). We build up ourselves on our faith by meditating upon its substance or contents (Ps. 1:2; Luke 2:19), by believing and appropriating it, by applying it to ourselves, and by being governed by it. Observe that it is a "most holy faith," for it both requires and promotes personal holiness. Thereby do we distinguish ourselves from carnal professors and apostates. "Praying in the Holy Ghost." We are to fervently and constantly seek His presence and Divine energy, which can supply us with the strength of will and affections that are necessary in order to comply with these precepts.

"Keep yourselves in the love of God" (v. 21). See to it that your love for Him is preserved in a pure, healthy, and vigorous condition. See to it that your love to Christ is in constant exercise by rendering obedience to Him who said, "If ye love me, keep my commandments" (John 14:15). "Keep thy *heart* with all diligence" (Prov. 4:23, ital. mine), for if your affections wane, your communion with Him will deteriorate and your witness for Him will be marred. Only as you keep yourselves in the love of God will you be distinguished from the carnal professors all around you. This exhortation is no needless one. The Christian is living in a world whose icy blasts will soon chill his love for God unless he guards it as the apple of his eye. A malicious adversary will do all he can to pour cold water upon it. Remember the solemn warning of Revelation 2:4. Oh, that Christ may never have to complain of you or me, "I have somewhat against thee, because thou hast *left* thy first love" (ital. mine). Rather, may our love "abound yet more and more" (Phil. 1:9). In order thereto *hope* must be in exercise, "looking for the mercy of our Lord Jesus Christ unto eternal life" (v. 21). Verses 22 and 23 make known our duty, and what is to be our attitude, toward those of our brethren who have fallen by the way. Toward some we are to show compassion, who by reason of tenderness can stand only mild rebukes and admonitions; whereas roughness would only drive them to despair and the postponement of their penitent looking to Christ. But others, who differ by temperament, or by reason of hardness of heart, require strong rebukes for their recovery, with frightening warnings concerning God's judgment against obstinate sinners who hold out against His threats and overtures of mercy. These we are to "save with fear, pulling them out of the fire; hating even the garment spotted by the flesh."

12

Jude 24, 25

Part 2

"Now unto him that is able to keep you from falling." In further consideration of the *connection* of this prayer, the following question is crucial: *who are* the ones that the Lord Jesus thus preserves? Not everyone who professes to believe and to be a follower of His, as is clear from the case of Judas Iscariot, is preserved by God from apostasy. Then whom does He preserve? Without doubt God preserves those who make a genuine effort to obey the exhortations found in verses 20-23, which were discussed at the end of the preceding chapter. These *true* believers, so far from being content with their present knowledge and spiritual attainments, sincerely endeavor to continue building up themselves on their most holy faith. These true lovers of God, so far from being indifferent to the state of their hearts, jealously watch their affections, in order that their love toward God might be preserved in a pure, healthy, and vigorous condition by regular exercise in acts of devotion and obedience. These true saints, so far from taking pleasure in flirting with the world and indulging their carnal lusts, have their hearts

engaged in "hating even the garment spotted by the flesh."
These true disciples pray fervently for the assistance of
the Holy Spirit in the performance of all their duties, and
are deeply solicitous about the welfare of their brothers
and sisters in Christ. *Such* are the ones who will, despite
all their weakness and frailties, be preserved by the power
and grace of God from apostasy.

Two Principles of Interpretation Necessary for Understanding This Prayer

It is of vital importance to a sound knowledge of Scripture that we observe the *order* in which truth is therein
set forth. For example, we find David saying, "Depart
from me, ye evildoers: for I will keep the commandments
of my God." This he said *before* praying the following
prayer: "Uphold me according unto Thy word" (Ps.
119:115, 116). There would have been no sincerity in praying for God to support him unless he had already resolved
to obey the Divine precepts. It is horrible mockery for
anyone to ask God to sustain him in a course of self-will.
First must come a holy purposing and resolution on our
part, and then the seeking of enabling grace. It is of equal
importance to a right understanding of Scripture that we
take special care not to separate what God has joined
together by detaching a sentence from its qualifying context. We often read the quotation, "My sheep shall never
perish." While that is substantially correct, those are not
the precise words Christ used. This is what He actually
said: "My sheep hear [heed!] my voice, and I know [ap-
prove] them, and they *follow Me* [contrary to their natural
inclinations]: And I give unto them eternal life; and *they*
[the heedful and obedient ones] shall never perish" (John
10:27, 28, brackets and ital. mine).

Faith Is the Instrumental Means of Our Preservation

"Now unto him that is able to keep you from falling." In these words we discover the *first* great *reason* behind the Apostle Jude's prayer, namely, the Divine ability to preserve the saints from apostasy. The discerning reader will perceive in the above remarks that the question of *how* Christ preserves His people has been anticipated and answered. He does so in a manner very different from that in which He keeps the planets in their courses, which He does by physical energy. Christ preserves His own by spiritual power, by the effectual operations of His grace within their souls. Christ preserves His people not in a course of reckless self-pleasing, but in one of self-denial. He preserves them by moving them to heed His warnings, to practice His precepts, and to follow the example that He has left them. He preserves them by enabling them to persevere in faith and holiness. We who are His are "kept by the power of God *through faith*" (I Peter 1:5, ital. mine), and faith has respect to His commandments (Ps. 119:66; Heb. 11:8) as well as to His promises. Christ indeed is "the author and finisher of our faith" (Heb. 12:2), yet *we* are the ones who must exercise that faith and not He. Yet, by the Holy Spirit, He is working in us "both to will and *to do* of his good pleasure" (Phil. 2:13). Just as faith is the instrumental means by which we are justified before God, our perseverance in faith is the instrumental means by which Christ preserves us until His coming (I Thess. 5:23; Jude 1).

After exhorting the saints as to their duties (vv. 20-23), Jude then intimates to whom they must look for their enablement and for blessing upon their endeavors: "unto him that is able to keep you from falling." His readers must place the whole of their dependence for preservation on the Lord Jesus. He does not say this in order to check their industry, but rather to encourage their hope of success. It is a great relief to faith to know that "God is able to make him [us] stand" (Rom. 14:4). John Gill begins his comments on Jude 24 by saying, "The people of God are *liable* to fall into temptation, into sin, into errors . . . and even into final and *total apostasy*, were it not for Divine power." Yea, they are painfully sensible both of their evil proclivities and their frailty, and therefore do they frequently cry to the Lord, "Hold thou me up, and I shall be safe: and I will have respect unto thy statutes continually" (Ps. 119:117). As they read of Adam in a state of innocency being unable to keep himself from falling, and likewise the angels in heaven, they know full well that imperfect and sinful creatures such as they are cannot keep themselves. The way to heaven is a narrow one, and there are precipices on either side. There are foes within and without seeking my destruction, and I have no more strength of my own than poor Peter had when he was put to the test by a maid.

Metaphors Describing the Inherent Weakness of Christians Are Meant to Direct Our Faith to God

Almost every figure used in the Bible to describe a child of God emphasizes his weakness and helplessness: a sheep, a branch of the vine, a bruised reed, smoking flax. It is only as we experientially discover our weakness that we learn to prize more highly the One who is able to keep us from falling. Is one of my readers tremblingly saying, "I fear that I too may perish in the wilderness"? Not so, if your prayer be sincere when you cry, "Hold up my goings in thy paths, that my footsteps slip not" (Ps. 17:5). Christ is able to protect you, because His power is limitless and

His grace boundless. What strength this should give the wearied warrior! David comforted himself therewith when he declared, "I will fear no evil: for thou art with me" (Ps. 23:4). There is a twofolk safeguarding of the elect spoken of in this Epistle: the one before regeneration, and the other after. In the opening verse of Jude they are spoken of as "sanctified by God the Father, and preserved in Jesus Christ, and called." They were set apart to salvation by the Father in His eternal decree (II Thess. 2:13), and "preserved" *before* they were effectually called. A wonderful and blessed fact is that! Even while wandering from the fold, yea, even while they were despising the Shepherd of their souls, His love watched over them (Jer. 31:3) and His power delivered them from an untimely grave. Death cannot seize an elect sinner until he has been born again!

Christ Does Not Raise Our Hopes Merely to Dash Them

What has just been pointed out should make it very evident that there is no question whatever about the Lord's *willingness* to preserve His people. If He has kept them from natural death while in a state of unregeneracy, much more will He deliver them from spiritual death now that He has made them new creatures (cf. Rom. 5:9, 10). If Christ were not *willing* to "make all grace abound" toward His people (II Cor. 9:8), to "keep that which I [they] have committed unto him against that day" (II Tim. 1:12, brackets mine), to "succor them that are tempted" (Heb. 2:18), and to "save them to the uttermost that come unto God by him" (Heb. 7:25), He most certainly would not tantalize them by affirming in each passage that He is *able* to do these things. When Christ asked the two blind men, who besought Him to have mercy upon them, "Believe ye that I am able to do this?" (Matt. 9:28), He was not raising a doubt in their minds as to His readiness to give them sight; but He was evoking their faith, as the next verse makes evident. The words "unto him that is *able* to keep you from falling" is a general expression including not only His might and willingness, but His goodness and munificence, which He has already brought, and shall continue to bring, to bear for the preservation of His people.

Christ Is Bound by Covenant Obligation to Preserve His People from Total, Final Apostasy

It is indeed true that the power of Christ is far greater than what He actually exercises, for His power is infinite. Were He so disposed, He could keep His people altogether from sin; but for wise and holy reasons He does not. As His forerunner John the Baptist declared to the Pharisees and Sadducees, "God is able of these stones to raise up children unto Abraham" (Matt. 3:9), so Christ could have commanded a legion of angels to deliver Him from His enemies (Matt. 26:53), but He would not. The exercise of His power was and is regulated by God's eternal purpose; He puts it forth only so far as He has stipulated to do so by covenant engagement. Thus the words "unto him that is able to keep you *from falling*" have reference not to every kind of falling, but from falling prey to the fatal errors of those "ungodly men" mentioned in verse 4, from being led astray by the sophistries and examples of heretical teachers. As the Shepherd of God's sheep, Christ has received a charge to preserve them: not from straying, but from destruction. It is the gross sins spoken of in the context, when joined with obstinacy and impenitence, from which Christ delivers His people. These are "presumptuous sins" (Ps. 19:13), which, if one continues in impenitent, are unpardonable sins (just like suicide). In other words, it is from total and final apostasy that Christ keeps all His own.

As an almighty Savior, Christ has been charged with the work of preserving His people. They were given to Him by the Father with that end in view. He is in every way qualified for the task considering both His Deity and His humanity (Heb. 2:18). All authority has been given to Him in heaven and earth (Matt. 28:18). He is as willing as He is competent, for it is the Father's will that He should lose none of His people (John 6:39), and therein He delights. He has a personal interest in them, for He has bought them for Himself. He is accountable for their custody. He therefore preserves them from being devoured by sin. No feeble Savior is ours, but rather One that is clothed with omnipotence. That was made manifest even during the days of His humiliation, when He cast out demons, healed the sick, and stilled the tempest by His authoritative fiat. It was evidenced when by a single utterance He caused those who came to arrest Him to fall backward to the ground (John 18:6). It was supremely demonstrated in His personal victory over death and the grave. That same almighty power is exercised in ordering all the affairs of His people, and in continually directing their wills and actions throughout the whole of their earthly pilgrimage. Of His vineyard He declares, "I the Lord do keep it; I will water it every moment: lest any hurt it, I will keep it night and day (Isa. 27:3).

The Glorious Reception with Which Christ Receives and Presents the Redeemed

"And to present you faultless before the presence of his glory with exceeding joy." Here is the *second reason* that

prompted this outburst of adoration. Christ not only pro-
tects His people here, but has provided for their felicity
hereafter. Such is His grace and power that He makes
good to them all that God has purposed and promised.
The *presentation* of His people to Himself is both individual and corporate. The former is at death, when He takes
the believer to Himself. Inexpressibly blessed is this: upon
its dismissal from the body the spirit of the believer is
conducted into the immediate presence of God, and the
Savior Himself admits it into heaven and presents it before the throne. The disembodied spirit, rid of all corruption and defilement, is received by Christ to the glory
of God. He will set that redeemed spirit of a justified sinner made perfect (Heb. 12:23) before Himself with great
complacence of heart, so that it will reflect His own perfections. He will advance it to the highest honor, fill it
with glory, express to it the uttermost of His love, and
behold it with delight. Christ receives each blood-washed
spirit at death to His everlasting embraces, and presents
it before the presence of His glory with exceeding joy.

Our present passage also looks forward to the time when
Christ will publicly present His people corporately to
Himself, when the Head and Savior who "loved the church,
and gave himself for it " will "present it to himself a glorious church, not having spot, or wrinkle, or any such thing;
but that it should be holy and without blemish" (Eph. 5:25,
27). This shall be the certain and triumphant result of His
love, as it shall be the consummation of our redemption.
The Greek word for *present* (No. 2476 in Strong and Thayer;
cf. *present*, 3936, in Eph. 5:27) can be used in the sense *to
set alongside of*. Having cleansed the Church from all her
natural pollution and prepared and adorned her for her
destined place as the companion of His glory, He will, formally, and officially, take her to Himself. This jubilant dec-

laration shall go forth: "Let us be glad and rejoice, and give honour to him [God]: for the marriage of the Lamb is come" (Rev. 19:7, brackets mine). Christ will have made the Church comely with His own perfections, and she will be full of beauty and splendor, like a bride adorned for her husband. He will then say, "Thou art all fair, my love; there is no spot in thee" (Song of Sol. 4:7). She shall be "all glorious within: her clothing is [shall be] of wrought gold." Of her it is said, "So shall the king greatly desire thy beauty" (Ps. 45:11, 13, brackets mine), and He shall be forever the satisfying Portion of her joy.

The Scriptures also indicate that on the resurrection morn Christ shall also present the Church to His Father (II Cor. 4:14), and shall say exultantly, "Behold I and the children which God hath given me" (Heb. 2:13; cf. Gen. 33:5; Isa. 8:18). Not one shall be lost (John 6:39, 40; 10:27-30; 17:12, 24)! And all shall be perfectly conformed to His holy image (Rom. 8:29). He will present us before God for His inspection, acceptance, and approbation. Says Albert Barnes,

> He will present us in the court of heaven, before the throne of the eternal Father, as His ransomed people, as recovered from the ruins of the fall, as saved by the merits of His blood. They shall not only be raised from the dead by Him, but publicly and solemnly presented to God as His, as recovered to His service and as having a title in the covenant of grace to the blessedness of heaven.

It is Christ taking His place before God as the triumphant Mediator, owning the "children" as God's gift to Him, confessing His oneness with them, and delighting in the fruits of His work. He presents them "faultless": justified, sanctified, glorified. The manner in which He does so will be "with exceeding joy," for He shall then "see of the travail of his soul, and shall be satisfied" (Isa. 53:11). In

Jude 15 we learn of the doom awaiting the apostates; here we behold the bliss appointed to the redeemed. They shall forever shine in Christ's righteousness, and He shall find His complacency in the Church as the partner of His blessedness.

A Doxology of Grand Ascription Directed to a Divine Person of Infinite Perfections

"To the only wise God our Saviour, be glory and majesty, dominion and power, both now and ever. Amen." We come to a consideration of the *nature and Object* of this prayer. It is a *doxology*, an expression of praise; and though it is brief, the Divine verities upon which it focuses are immense. Seeing that the Lord is arrayed with glory and beauty (Job 40:10), we should continually ascribe these excellencies to Him (Exod. 15:11; I Chron. 29:11). The saints are to publish and proclaim the perfections of their God: "Sing forth the honour of his name: make his praise glorious" (Ps. 66:2). This is what the apostles did, and we should emulate them. Here He is adored for His wisdom. There is something here that may present a difficulty to young theologians who have learned to distinguish between the incommunicable attributes of God, such as His infinitude and immutability, and His communicable attributes, such as mercy, wisdom, and so forth. Seeing that God has endowed some of His creatures with wisdom, how can He be said to be *"only* wise"? First, He is *superlatively* wise. His wisdom is so vastly superior to that of men and angels that their creaturely wisdom is foolishness by comparison. Secondly, He is *essentially* wise. God's wisdom is not a quality separate from Himself as ours is. There are many men who are far from being wise men; but God would not be God if He were not omniscient, being naturally endowed with all knowledge and Himself the very Fountainhead of all wisdom. Thirdly, He is *originally* wise, without derivation. All wisdom is *from* God, because He possesses all wisdom *in* Himself. All the true wisdom of creatures is but a ray from His light.

The glorious *Object* of this doxology is none other than the *Mediator* of the covenant of grace. The reasons for so honoring Him are the omnipotence and omniscience that He possesses, which are gloriously displayed in His saving of the Church. In view of what is predicated of Him in verse 24, there should not be the slightest doubt in our minds that "the only wise God" of verse 25 is none other than the Lord Jesus Christ, for it is His particular province as the Shepherd to preserve His Church from destruction and to present it in glory to the Father. Furthermore, the added epithet, "God our Saviour," confirms the matter. Here absolute Deity is ascribed to Him: "the only wise *God*," as it also is in Titus 2:13 (where the Greek text would more accurately and literally be rendered, "the great God and Saviour of us, Jesus Christ"), II Peter 1:1 (where the Greek should be translated, "of our God and Saviour Jesus Christ," witness the marginal notes of the KJV and ASV), and many other places. Christ the Son is "the only wise God," though not to the exclusion of the Father and the Spirit. Probably He is here designated as such in designed contrast with the false and foolish "gods" of the heretical corruptors mentioned in the context. I might add that by comparison to the sovereign triune God of Holy Writ, who is most gloriously represented in the God-man Jesus the Christ (who now reigns as the absolute Lord of the universe), the fictitious God of the Unitarians, of twentieth-century Modernists, and of most Arminians is also foolish and puerile.

Christ's Unique Fitness for the Work Assigned to Him

It is the strength and sufficiency of Christ for all the concerns of His redemptive mediation that is here magnified. He is adored as the One who will triumphantly complete the work given Him to do, a work that no mere creature, no, not even an archangel, could accomplish. None but One who is both God and man could act as Mediator. None but a Divine Person could offer an adequate satisfaction to Divine justice. None but one possessed of infinite merit could provide a sacrifice of infinite value. None but God could preserve sheep in the midst of wolves. In Proverbs 8, especially verses 12, 13, 31, and 32, Christ is denominated "wisdom," and is heard speaking as a distinct Person. He was heralded as the "Wonderful Counsellor" (Isa. 9:6). He designated Himself "wisdom" in Luke 7:35. He is expressly called "the wisdom of God" (I Cor. 1:24), "In whom are hid all the treasures of wisdom and knowledge" (Col. 2:3). His wisdom appears in His creating all things (John 1:3), in His governing and maintaining all things (Heb. 1:3), and in that the Father "hath committed all judgment unto the Son" (John 5:22).

The consummate wisdom of Christ was manifested during the days of His flesh. He opened to men the secrets of God (Matt. 13:11). He declared, "The Son can do nothing of himself [which in the light of the context following means that He does nothing independently of the Father's will], but what he seeth the Father do: for what things soever He doeth, these also doeth *the Son* likewise" (John 5:19, 30 brackets and ital. mine). Christ thereby affirmed an equality of competency between Himself and His Father. He "needed not that any should testify of man: for he knew what was in man" (John 2:25). Those who heard Him teach "were astonished, and said, Whence hath this man this wisdom, and these mighty works?" (Matt. 13:54). Christ's unique wisdom appeared in answering and silencing His enemies. "Never man spake like this man" (John 7:46), testified those sent to arrest Him. He so confounded His critics that at the end Matthew testified, "neither durst any man from that day forth ask him any more questions" (Matt. 22:46). Since, therefore, He is endowed with omniscience, let us find no fault with any of His dealings with us. Let us rather take to Him all our problems; let us confide absolutely in Him, putting ourselves and all our affairs into His hands.

The Highest Praise Is Due the Lord Christ

Since He *is* "the only wise God our Saviour"—the sole, sufficient, and successful Savior—let us laud Him as such. As those in heaven cast their crowns before the Lamb and extol His peerless perfections, so should we who are still upon earth. Since Christ subjected Himself to such unspeakable dishonor and abasement for our sakes, yea, enduring suffering to death itself, and that the death of the cross, how readily and heartily should we honor and magnify Him, crying with the apostle, "Unto him be glory and majesty, dominion and power"! *Glory* is the displaying of excellence in such a way that gains approbation from all who behold it. Here the word signifies the high honor and esteem that is due to Christ because of His perfections, whereby He infinitely surpasses all creatures and things. *Majesty* refers to His exalted dignity and Divine greatness that make Him to be honored and preferred beyond all His creatures, having received a name that is above every name (Phil. 2:9). *Dominion* is that absolute rule or ownership that is gained by conquest and maintained by strength or might superior to that of all rivals. This the

God-man exercises in such a way that "none can stay his hand, or say unto him, What doest thou?" (Dan. 4:35). He has already crushed the head of Satan, His most powerful enemy (Gen. 3:15), and thrown his evil kingdom into chaos. "And having spoiled principalities and powers, he made a shew of them openly, triumphing over them" in His death on the cross (Col. 2:15). *Power* here means that authority to rule which is derived from legal right. Because Christ "became obedient unto death, even the death of the cross" (Phil. 2:8, 9), God the Father has exalted Him to the place of universal authority and rule (Matt. 28:18) where He now reigns as "KING OF KINGS AND LORD OF LORDS" (Rev. 19:16). This universal rule Christ *earned* as a legal right by His perfect obedience as the second Adam (Gen. 1:26-28). As the God-man, Christ not only merits authority and dominion over the earth with all of its creatures but also over the entire universe that He Himself created.

King Jesus Reigns Both Now and Forever

"To the only wise God our Saviour, be glory and majesty, dominion and power, *both now* and ever. Amen." Note well the two words set in italics. Radically different was the inspired concept of Jude from that of so many "students of prophecy" who postpone Christ's reign to some future "millenial" era. It is both the present and the endless dignities of the Mediator that are here in view. He has *already* been "crowned with glory and honour" (Heb. 2:9). Majesty is His today, for He is exalted "Far above all principality, and power," for God "*hath* [not "will"!] put all things under his feet" (Eph. 1:21, 22, ital. and brackets mine). Dominion is also exercised by Him now, and in the strength by which He obtained dominion He is presently "upholding all things by the word of his power" (Heb. 1:3). Even now the Lord Jesus is seated upon the throne of David (Acts 2:29-35), "angels and authorities and powers being made [having been] made subject unto him." (I Peter 3:22). So shall He reign, not merely for a thousand years, but *forever*. Amen. Thus does Jude conclude the most solemn of all Epistles with this paean of holy exultation over the present and eternal glory of the Lamb.

13
Revelation 1:5, 6
Part 1

The prayer now before us really forms the closing part of the salutation and benediction of verses 4 and 5 of Revelation 1, in which "grace and peace" are sought from the triune God in His distinct persons: (1) "from him which is, and which was, and which is to come," that is, from Jehovah as the self-existing and immutable One—He is addressed by the equivalent of His memorial name (Exod. 3:13-17) by which His eternal being and covenant-keeping faithfulness were to be remembered (Exod. 6:2-5; "the LORD" equals "Jehovah" throughout the Old Testament); (2) "from the seven Spirits which are before his throne," that is, from the Holy Spirit in the fullness of His power and diversity of His operations (Isa. 11:1, 2); and (3) "from Jesus Christ," who is mentioned last as the connecting Link between God and His people. A threefold appellation is here accorded the Savior: (1) "the faithful witness," which contemplates and covers the whole of His virtuous life from the manger to the cross; (2) "the first begotten [better, "Firstborn"] of the dead," (brackets mine) which celebrates His victory over the tomb—this is a title of dignity (Gen. 49:3), and signifies priority of *rank* rather than time; and (3) "and the prince of the kings of the earth," which announces His regal majesty and dominion. This third title views the Conqueror as exalted "Far above all principality, and power" (Eph. 1:21), as the One upon whose shoulder the government of the universe has been laid (Isa. 9:6), who is even now "upholding all things by the word of his power" (Heb. 1:3), and before whom every knee shall yet bow (Phil. 2:10).

An Analytical Synopsis of the Prayer

The preceding recital of the Redeemer's perfections and dignities evoked from the mouth of the Apostle John this adoring exclamation: "Unto him that loved us, and washed us from our sins in his own blood, And hath made us kings and priests unto God and his Father; to him be glory and dominion for ever and ever. Amen." Thus the *nature* of our prayer is again a doxology. Its *Object* is the Son of God incarnate in His mediatorial character and office. Its *adorers* are those of "us" who are the beneficiaries of His mediation. Its inciting *reasons* are our apprehensions of His unfathomable love, the cleansing efficacy of His precious blood, and the wondrous dignities that He has conferred upon His redeemed. Its *ascription* is "to him be glory and dominion," not merely for a thousand years, but "for ever and ever," which closes with the assuring affirmation, "Amen"—it shall be so. For the benefit of young preachers I shall add a few more remarks on doxologies in general.

The Doxologies Are Needed to Enlarge Our Conceptions of the Persons of the Godhead

The doxologies of Scripture reveal our need to form more exalted conceptions of the Divine Persons. In order to do so, we must engage in more frequent and devout meditations on their ineffable attributes. How little do our thoughts dwell upon the display of them in the material creation. Divinity is "clearly seen" in the things that God has made, and even the heathen are charged with inexcusable guilt because of their failure to glorify God for His handiwork (Rom. 1:19-21). Not only should our senses be regaled by the lovely colors of the trees and perfumes of the flowers, but our minds ought to dwell upon the motions and instincts of animals, admiring the Divine hand that so equipped them. How little do we reflect on the marvels of our own bodies, the structure, convenience, and perfect adaptedness of each member. How few unite with the Psalmist in exclaiming, "I will praise thee; for I am fearfully and wonderfully made: marvellous are thy works; and that my soul knoweth right well" (Ps. 139:14). How much more wonderful are the faculties of our inner man, raising us high above all irrational creatures. How better can our reason be employed than in extolling the One who has so richly endowed us? Yet how little grateful acknowledgment is made to the beneficent Fashioner and Donor of our beings.

How little do we consider the wisdom and power of God as manifested in the *government* of the world. Let us take, for example, the balance preserved between the sexes in the relative number of births and deaths, so that the population of the earth is maintained from generation to generation without any human contriving. Or let us take into account the various temperaments and talents given to men, so that some are wise for counsel, administration and management, some are better qualified for hard manual labor, and others to serve in clerical functions. Or consider how His government curbs the baser passions of men, so that such a measure of law and order obtains

generally in society that the weak are not destroyed by
the strong nor the good unable to live in a world that
wholly "lieth in wickedness" (I John 5:19). Or think how
God sets bounds to the success of rapacious dictators, so
that when it appears they are on the very point of carrying
all before them, they are suddenly stopped by the One
who has decreed that they shall go "no farther." Or ponder how, in His application of the law of retribution, individuals and nations are made to reap what they sow,
whether it be good or evil. It is because we pay so little
attention to these and a hundred other similar phenom-
ena that we are so rarely moved to cry, "Alleluia: for the
Lord God omnipotent reigneth" (Rev. 19:6).

Doxologies Are Wholly Devoted to the Praises of Deity, Particularly to the Works of Divine Grace

But it is the wondrous works of God in the realm of
grace, rather than in creation and providence, that are
most calculated to draw out the hearts of God's people in
adoring homage. More particularly, those works wherein
the Darling of His own heart was and is engaged on our
behalf draw forth our admiration and praise. Thus it is
in the verses we are now pondering. No sooner was the
peerless Person and perfections of the eternal Lover of his
soul set before the mind and heart of the Apostle John
than that he cried exultantly, "To Him be glory and dominion for ever and ever." And thus it is with all of God's
true saints. Such a cry is the spontaneous response and
outgoing of their souls to Him. That leads me to point out
the one thing that is common to all doxologies: in them
praise is always offered exclusively to Deity, and never to
any mere human agency or accomplishment. Self-occu-
pation and self-gratulation have no place whatever in

them. Different far is that from the low level of spirituality generally prevailing in the churches today. This writer was once present at a service where a hymn was sung, the chorus of which ran, "Oh, how I love Jesus." But I could not conscientiously join in singing it. None in heaven are guilty of lauding themselves or magnifying their graces, nor should any Christians do so here upon earth.

The Particular Object of this Doxology

The *Object* of this adoration and thanksgiving is that Blessed One who undertook, with the Father and the Spirit, to save His people from all their sins and miseries by the price of His blood and the arm of His power. In His essential Person, God the Son is co-equal and co-eternal with the Father and the Spirit "who is over all, God blessed for ever. Amen" (Rom. 9:5). He is the uncreated Sun of righteousness (Ps. 84:11; Mal. 4:2). In Him all the glory of the Godhead shines forth, and by Him all the perfections of Deity have been manifested. In response to this very homage, He declares, "I am Alpha and Omega, the beginning and ending, saith the Lord, which is, and which was, and which is to come, the Almighty" (Rev. 1:8). Before the worlds were made He entered into covenant engagement to become incarnate, to be made in the likeness of sinful flesh (Rom. 8:3) to serve as the Surety of His people, to be the Bridegroom of His Church—its complete and all-sufficient Savior. As such He is the Man of God's right hand, the Fellow of the Lord of hosts, the King of glory. His work is honorable, His fullness infinite, His power omnipotent. His throne is for ever and ever. His name is above every name. His glory is above the heavens. It is impossible to extol Him too highly, for His glorious name "is exalted *above all* blessing and praise" (Neh. 9:5, ital. mine).

In the immediate context this adorable One is viewed in His *theanthropic* person, as incarnate, as the God-man Mediator. He is set forth in His threefold office as Prophet, Priest, and Potentate. His prophetical office is clearly denoted in the title "the faithful Witness," for in Old Testament prophecy the Father announced, "I have given him for a witness to the people" (Isa. 55:4). Christ Himself declared to Pilate, "To this end was I born, and for this cause came I into the world, that I should bear witness unto the truth" (John 18:37). As such He proclaimed the Gospel to the poor and confirmed it by mighty miracles. His sacerdotal office is necessarily implied in the expression "first begotten of the dead," for in death He offered Himself as a sacrifice to God to make satisfaction for the transgressions of His people. He then rose again that He might continue to exercise His priesthood by His constant intercession for them. His regal office appears plainly in the designation "prince of the kings of the earth," for He has absolute dominion over them. By Him they reign (Prov. 8:15), and to Him they are commanded to render allegiance (Ps. 2:10-12). To Him we are to hearken, in Him we are to believe, and to Him we are to be subject. Singly and collectively these titles announce that He is to be greatly respected and revered.

Angels Are Filled with Wonder over the Redeeming Love of Christ for His Church

While an exile on the isle of Patmos, John was engaged in contemplating Immanuel in the excellencies of His Person, offices, and work. As he did so his heart was enraptured, and he exclaimed, "Unto him that loved us." The love of Christ is here expressed by the Apostle John in the *past* tense, not because it is inoperative in the present but to focus our attention upon its earlier exercises. The love of Christ is the grandest fact and mystery revealed in Holy Writ. That love originated in His heart and was in operation for all eternity, for before the mountains were formed His "delights were with the sons of men" (Prov. 8:31). That wonderful love was put forth by Christ in connection with the everlasting covenant, wherein He agreed to serve as the Sponsor of His people and to discharge all their obligations. That He should take complacence in creatures of the dust is the marvel of heaven (Eph. 3:8-10; I Peter 1:12). That He should set His heart upon them while viewed in their fallen estate is incomprehensible. That love was expressed openly in His incarnation, humiliation, obedience, sufferings, and death.

Holy Scripture declares that "the love of Christ ... passeth knowledge" (Eph. 3:19). It is entirely beyond finite computation or comprehension. That the Son of God should ever deign to *notice* finite creatures was an act of great condescension on His part (Ps. 13:6). That he should go so far as to *pity* them is yet more wonderful. That He should *love* us in our pollution entirely transcends our understanding. That the outgoings of His heart toward the Church moved Him to lay aside the glory that He had with the Father before the world was (John 17:5), to take upon Him the form of a servant, and to become "obedient unto death" for their sakes, "even the death of the cross" (Phil. 2:7, 8), surmounts all thought and is beyond all praise. That the Holy One should be willing to be made sin for His people (II Cor. 5:21) and to endure the curse that endless blessing should be their portion (Gal. 3:13, 14) is altogether inconceivable. As S. E. Pierce so ably expressed it,

His love is one perfect and continued act from everlasting to everlasting. It knows no abatement or decay. It is eternal and immutable love. It exceeds all conception and surpasses all expression. To give the utmost proof of it, "Christ died for the ungodly" (Rom. 5:6). In His life He fully displayed His love. In His sufferings and death He stamped it with an everlasting emphasis.

Christ's Love Is Completely Impartial, Not Evoked by Any Merit in Its Objects

The love of Christ was an entirely disinterested love, for it was uninfluenced by anything in its objects or any other considerations external to Himself. There was nothing whatever in His people, either actual or foreseen, to call His love into exercise: nothing actual, for they had rebelled against God and had deliberately chosen as their exemplar and master one who was a liar and murderer from the beginning; nothing foreseen, for no excellence could they bear but that which His own gracious hand wrought in them. The love of Christ infinitely excelled in purity, in intensity, in its disinterestedness, any that ever moved in a human breast. It was altogether free and spontaneous. He loved us when we were loveless and unlovely. We were entirely unable to render Him any proper compensation or return. His own essential blessedness and glory could neither be diminished by our damnation nor increased by our salvation. His love was uninvited, unattracted, altogether self-caused and self-motivated. It was His love that stirred every other attribute—His wisdom, power, holiness, and so forth—to activity. The words of David, "he delivered me, *because* he delighted in me" (Ps. 18:19, ital. mine), provide the Divine explanation of my redemption.

The love of Christ was a *discriminating* one. "The Lord

is good to all: and his tender mercies are over all his works" (Ps. 145:9). He is benevolent toward all His creatures, making His sun to rise on the evil and the good, and sending rain on the just and on the unjust (Matt. 5:45). "He is *kind* unto the unthankful and to the evil" (Luke 6:35, ital. mine). But Christ *loved* the Church and gave Himself for it with a love such as He does not bear toward all mankind. The Church is the one special and peculiar object of His affections. For her He reserves and entertains a unique love and devotion that makes her shine among all the created works of His hands with the unmistakable radiance of a favorite. Husbands are bidden to love their wives "even as Christ also loved the church" (Eph. 5:25). The love of a husband toward his wife is a special and exclusive one; so Christ cherishes for His Church a particular affection. It is set upon His Bride rather than upon the human race at large. She is His peculiar treasure. "Having loved *his own* which were in the world, he loved them unto the end" (John 13:1, ital. mine). Instead of caviling at this truth, let us enjoy its preciousness. Christ's love is also a constant and durable one, exercised upon its objects "unto the end"; and, as we shall now see, it is a sacrificial and enriching love.

Christ's Love Addressed Itself to Our Greatest Need: The Purging of Our Sins

The *manifestations* of Christ's love correspond to our woe and want, its operations being suited to the condition and circumstances of its objects. Our direst need was the putting away of our sins, and that need has been fully met by Him. His love alone could not remove our transgressions "as far as the east is from the west." The claims of God had to be met; the penalty of the Law had to be endured. "Without shedding of blood is no remission" (Heb. 9:22), and Christ so loved the Church as to shed His precious blood for her. Hence the Apostle John is here heard exclaiming, "Unto him that loved us, and washed us from our sins in [or "by"] his own blood." This is the second inspiring reason or motive behind this benediction. This reference to the blood of Christ necessarily underscores His Deity as well as His humanity. None but a creature can shed blood and die, but none but God can forgive sins. It is likewise a witness to the vicarious or substitutionary nature and efficacy of His sacrifice. How otherwise could it wash us from our sins? Moreover, it celebrates the supreme proof of His care for His people. "Love is strong as death; . . . Many waters cannot quench love, neither can the flood drown it" (Song of Sol. 8:6, 7) demonstrated at the cross, where all the waves and billows of God's wrath (Ps. 42:7) went over the Sinbearer.

The surpassing love of Christ was evidenced by His espousing the persons of God's elect, undertaking their cause, assuming their nature, obeying and suffering in their room and stead. The Apostle Paul brought this blessed truth home with application to believers when he said,

> Be ye therefore followers of God, as dear children; And walk in love, as Christ also hath loved us, and hath given himself for us an offering and a sacrifice to God for a sweetsmelling savour (Eph. 5:1, 2).

The Lord Jesus knew what was necessary for our deliverance, and His love prompted Him to the accomplishment of the same. And the apostles Paul and John understood and taught concerning the heavy debt of love and gratitude that is laid upon all the happy beneficiaries of Christ's saving work. To "wash us from our sins" was of the very essence of those things that are necessary for our salvation, and for that His blood must be shed. What stupendous proof was that of His love! Herein is love, that the Just should voluntarily and gladly suffer for the unjust, "that he might bring us to God" (I Peter 3:18). "But God commendeth his love toward us, in that, while we were yet sinners, Christ died for us" (Rom. 5:8). Amazing tidings, that Christ Jesus made full atonement for those who were at that very moment His enemies (Rom. 5:10)! He chose to lay down His life for those who were by nature and by practice rebels against God, rather than that they should be a sacrifice to the wrath of God forever. The guilty transgress, but the innocent One is condemned. The ungodly offend, but the Holy One endures the penalty. The servant commits the crime, but the Lord of glory blots it out. What reason have we to adore Him!

Christ's Love Is Infinite and Immutable

How can Christ ever manifest His love for His people in a way that exceeds that which He has already done? "Greater love hath no man than this, that a man lay down his life for his friends" (John 15:13). Yet this was the God-man, and by so doing He showed that His love was infinite and eternal—incapable of amplification! He shone forth in the full meridian power and splendor of His love in Gethsemane and on Calvary. There he sustained in His soul the whole of the awful curse that was due and payable to the sins of His people. Then it was that it pleased the Father to bruise Him and put His soul to grief (Isa. 53:10). His anguish was inconceivable. He cried out under it, "Why hast thou forsaken me?" It was *thus* that He loved us, and it was thereby that He provided the fountain to cleanse us from our iniquities. Through the shedding of His precious blood He has purged His people entirely from the guilt and defilement of sin. Let us join in the exultant praise of S. E. Pierce:

> Blessings, eternal blessings on the Lamb who bore our sins and carried our sorrows! His bloody sweat is our everlasting health and cure. His soul-travail is our everlasting deliverance from the curse of the Law and the wrath to come. His bearing our sins in His own body on the Tree is our everlasting discharge from them. His most precious bloodshedding is our everlasting purification.

"And washed us from our sins in his own blood." Sin alike stains our record before God, pollutes the soul, and defiles the conscience; and naught can remove it but the atoning and cleansing blood of Christ. Sin is the only thing that the Lord Jesus hates. It is essential to His holiness that He should do so. He hates it immutably, and can as soon cease to love God as love it. Nevertheless His love to His people is even greater than His hatred of sin. Through their fall in Adam they are sinners; their fallen natures are totally depraved. By thought, word, and deed they are sinners. They are guilty of literally countless transgressions, for their sins are more in number than the hairs of their heads (Ps. 40:12). Yet Christ loved them! He did so before they sinned in Adam, and His forethoughts of them in their fallen estate produced no change in His love for them; rather, they afforded greater opportunity for Him to display that love. Therefore He became incarnate, that He might blot out their sins. Nothing was more loathsome to the Holy One of God. Yet He was willing to be an alien to His mother's children, despised and rejected of men, mocked and scourged by them, yea, abandoned by God for a season, that His people might be cleansed.

Christ's Once-for-All Washing of His People

I fully agree with John Gill's comments on the words "washed us from our sins":

> This is not to be understood of the sanctification of their natures, which is the work of the Spirit, but of atonement for their sins and justification from them.

In other words, it is the purchase of redemption, and not its application, that is here in view. The latter, of course, follows at regeneration, for all whom He washed judicially from the guilt and penalty of sin (once for all at Golgotha) are in due time cleansed and released from the love and dominion of sin. That which is signified in the clause before us is guilt cancelled, condemnation removed, the curse of the Law taken away, and the sentence of acquittal pronounced. This is the portion of *all* believers: "There is therefore now no condemnation to them which are in Christ Jesus" (Rom. 8:1). We must distinguish between the justification of our *persons* once for all (Acts 13:39) and the pardon of those sins that we commit as Christians (I John 1:9). The latter must be penitentially confessed, and then we are forgiven and cleansed on the ground of Christ's blood. It is the former that is in view in Revelation 1:5, where the Apostle John is rejoicing in the love of Him whose blood has once and for all washed the *persons* of the saints. The ongoing cleansing from sin that is needed day by day is acknowledged in Revelation 7:13, 14, where we behold the saints in brilliant white robes, previously travel-stained *garments* that they had cleansed day by day (cf. John 13:3-17).

14

Revelation 1:5, 6

Part 2

Two evidences of the love of Christ for His people are mentioned in this prayer: His cleansing of them from their sins by His own blood, and His enriching of them by the dignities He bestows upon them. But there is also a third expression and manifestation of His love that, though not distinctly expressed, is necessarily implied here, namely, His *provision for* them. As the result of the work that His love prompted Him to perform on their behalf, He meritoriously secured the Holy Spirit for His people (Acts 2:33). Christ therefore sends the Holy Spirit to regenerate them, to take of the things of Christ and show the same to them (John 16:14, 15), to impart an experiential and saving knowledge of the Lord Jesus, and to produce faith in their hearts so that they believe on Him to everlasting life. I say that all of this is necessarily implied, for only by these realities are they enabled truly and feelingly to exclaim "unto him that loved *us*," yea, so that each of them may aver that this Christ the Son of God "loved *me*, and gave himself for me" (Gal. 2:20). This is the quintessence of real blessedness: to be assured by the Spirit from the Word that I am an object of Christ's infinite and immutable love. The knowledge thereof makes Him "altogether lovely" in my esteem (Song. of Sol. 5:16), rejoices my soul, and sanctifies my affections.

By Saving Faith, One Looks Outside Oneself to Christ

See here the appropriating nature of saving faith. It takes hold of Christ and His sacrifice for sinners as made known in the Word of truth. It says, Here is a love letter from heaven about the glorious Gospel of the Son of God, which gives an account of Christ's love and the strongest and greatest possible proofs thereof. I see that this letter is *for me*, for it is addressed to sinners, yea, to the very chief of sinners. It both invites and commands me to receive this Divine Lover to myself and to believe unfeignedly in the sufficiency of His atoning blood for *my* sins. Therefore I take Him as He is freely proffered by the Gospel, and rely on His own word: "him that cometh to me I will in no wise cast out" (John 6:37). This faith comes not by feelings of my love to Christ, but by the *hearing* of His love for sinners (Rom. 5:8; 10:17). True, the Holy Spirit, in the day of His power, makes impressions on the heart by the Word. Yet the *ground* of faith is not those impressions, but the Gospel itself. The *Object* of faith is not Christ working on the heart and softening it, but rather Christ as He is presented to our acceptance in the Word. What we are called upon to hear is not Christ speaking secretly within us, but Christ speaking openly, objectively, without us.

The Blessed Fruits of Saving Faith

A most dreadful curse is pronounced upon all who "love not the Lord Jesus Christ" (I Cor. 16:22). Solemn indeed is it to realize that that curse rests upon the vast majority of our fellows, even in those countries that are reputed to be Christian. But why does any sinner love Christ? One can only do so because he believes in the love of Christ toward sinners. He perceives the wonder and preciousness thereof; for "faith . . . worketh by love" (Gal. 5:6), even by the love of Christ manifested toward us. It receives or takes His love to the heart. Then it works peace in the conscience, gives conscious access to God (Eph. 3:12), stirs up joy in Him, and promotes communion with and conformity to Him. That faith, implanted by the Holy Spirit, that works by love—the reflex of our apprehension and appropriation of Christ's love—slays our enmity against God, and causes us to delight in His Law (Rom. 7:22). Such faith knows, on the authority of the Word of God, that our sins—which were the cause of our separation and alienation from Him—have been washed away by the atoning blood of Christ. How inexpressibly blessed it is to know that in the fullness of time Christ appeared "to put away sin by the sacrifice of himself" (Heb. 9:26) and that God says of all believers, "their sins and iniquities will I remember no more" (Heb. 10:17).

On our trust in the Divine testimonies of the Gospel depends, to a large extent, both our practical holiness and our comfort. Our love to Christ and adoration of Him will grow or diminish in proportion to our faith in the Person and work of Christ. Where there is a personal assurance of His love, there cannot but be a joining with the saints in heaven in praising Christ for washing us from our sins (Rev. 5:9, 10). But many will object, "I still have so much sin in me; and it so often gets the mastery over me, that I dare not cherish the assurance that Christ has washed me from *my* sins." If that be your case, I ask, Do you mourn over your corruptions, and earnestly desire to be forever rid of them? If so, that is proof that you are entitled to rejoice in Christ's atoning blood. God sees fit to leave sin in you, that in this life you may be kept humble before Him and marvel the more at His longsuffering. It is His appointment that the Lamb should now be eaten "with bitter herbs" (Exod. 12:8). This world is not the place of your rest. God suffers you to be harassed by your lusts, that you may look forward more eagerly to the deliverance and rest awaiting you. Though Romans 7:14-25 accurately describes your present experience, Romans 8:1 also declares, "There is therefore now no condemnation to them which are in Christ Jesus"!

The Exalted Positions and Privileges Enjoyed by Christians by Virtue of Union with Christ

"And hath made us kings and priests unto God and his Father." Here is the third inspiring reason for the ascription that follows. Having owned the indebtedness of the saints to the Savior's love and sacrifice, the Apostle John now celebrates, in the language of "the spirits of just men made perfect" (Rev. 5:10; Heb. 5:10), the high dignities that He has conferred upon them. We who are children of the most High, in due measure, are made partakers of the honors of Him who is both the King of kings and our great High Priest; and the apprehension of this fact evokes a song of praise to Him. As we realize that the Lord Jesus shares His own honors with His redeemed, conferring upon them both regal dignity and priestly nearness to God, we cannot but exultantly exclaim, "*To him* be glory and dominion for ever and ever." We were *virtually* made kings and priests when He contracted to fulfill the terms of the everlasting covenant, for by that engagement we were constituted such. *By purchase* we were made kings and priests when He paid the price of our redemption, for it was by His merits that He purchased these privileges for us. *Federally* we were made so when He ascended on high (Eph. 4:8; 2:6) and entered within the veil as our Forerunner (Heb. 6:19, 20). *Actually* we were made so at our regeneration, when we became participants in His anointing.

"And hath made us kings and priests unto God." Here we have the Redeemer exalting and ennobling His redeemed. This presupposes and follows upon our pardon, and is the *positive* result of Christ's meritorious obedience to God's Law (without which He could not have died in the place of sinners). The One who loved us has not only removed our defilements but has also restored us to the Divine favor and fellowship. Furthermore, he has secured for us a glorious reward; He took our place that we might share His. In order that we may be protected from certain insidious errors, which have brought not a few of God's children into bondage, it is important to perceive that these designations belong not merely to a very select and advanced class of Christians, but equally to *all* believers. It is also necessary, lest we be robbed by Dispensationalism, that we realize that these dignities pertain to us *now*. They are not postponed until our arrival in heaven, and still less till the dawn of the millennium. Every saint has these two honors conferred on him at once: he is a regal priest, and a priestly monarch. Herein we see the dignity and nobility of the Lord's people. The world looks upon us as mean and contemptible, but He speaks of us as "the excellent, in whom is all my delight" (Ps. 16:3).

When Paul states in II Corinthians 1:21 that God "stablisheth us . . . in Christ, and hath *anointed* us," (ital. mine) he is implying that God has made us kings and priests; for the word *anointed* is expressive of *dignity*.

Kings and priests were anointed when inaugurated in their offices. Therefore when it is said that God has anointed all who are in Christ Jesus, it intimates that He has qualified and authorized them to the discharge of these high offices. In drawing a sharp contrast between true believers and false brethren and false teachers, the Apostle John says, "But ye have an unction from the Holy One. . . . But the anointing which ye have received of him abideth in you" (I John 2:20, 27). We have a participation in Christ's anointing (Acts 10:38), receiving the same Spirit wherewith He was anointed (a beautiful type of Christ's anointing is set forth in Ps. 133:2). The blessedness of the elect appears in that they are made both kings and priests by virtue of the Name in which they are presented before God. They who "receive abundance of grace and of the gift of righteousness shall *reign* in life by one, Jesus Christ" (Rom. 5:17, ital. mine). Though in all things Christ has the preeminence, being "the King of kings"—for He has been "anointed . . . with the oil of gladness *above* thy [His] fellows" (Ps. 45:7, ital. and brackets mine)—yet His companions are invested with royalty; and "*as* he is, *so* are we in this world" (I John 4:17, ital. mine). Oh, for faith to appropriate that fact, and for grace to conduct ourselves accordingly!

Apparently there is a designed contrast between the two expressions, "the kings *of the earth*" and "hath made *us* kings and priests *unto God.*" They are kings naturally, we spiritually; they unto men, we unto God. They are merely kings, but we are both kings and priests. The dominion of earthly monarchs is but fleeting; their regal glory quickly fades. Even the glory of Solomon, which surpassed that of all the kings of the earth, was but of brief duration. But *we* shall be co-regents with a King the foundation of whose throne (Rev. 3:21) is indestructible, whose scepter is everlasting, and whose dominion is universal (Matt. 28:18; Rev. 21:7). We shall be clothed with immortality and vested with a glory that shall never be dimmed. Believers are *kings*, not in the sense that they take any part in heaven's rule over the earth, but as sharers in their Lord's triumph over Satan, sin, and the world. In *that* Christians are also distinguished from the *angels*. For they are not kings, nor will they ever reign, for they are not anointed. They have no union with the incarnate Son of God, and therefore they are not "joint-heirs with Christ" as the redeemed are (Rom. 8:17). So far from it, they are all "ministering spirits, sent forth to minister for them who shall be heirs of salvation" (Heb. 1:14). A subordinate place and a subservient task is *theirs*!

The Moral Dominion Exercised by the Christian

Christ has not only done a great work *for* His people, but He accomplishes a grand work *in* them. He not only washes them from their sins, which He hates, but He also transforms by His power their persons, which He loves. He does not leave them as He first finds them—under the dominion of Satan, sin, and the world. No, but He makes them *kings*. A king is one who is called to rule, who is invested with authority, and who exercises dominion; and so do believers over their enemies. True, some of the subjects we are called to rule are both strong and turbulent, yet we are "more than conquerors through him that loved us" (Rom. 8:37). The Christian is "a king, against whom there is no rising up" (Prov. 30:31). Though he may often be overcome in his person, yet he shall never be overcome in his cause. There is still a law in his members warring against the law of his mind (Rom. 8:23), yet sin shall not have dominion over him (Rom. 6:14). Once the world kept him in bondage, presuming to dictate his conduct, so that he was afraid to defy its customs and ashamed to ignore its maxims. But "whatsoever is born of God overcometh the world: and this is the victory that overcometh the world, even our faith" (I John 5:4). By God's gracious gift of faith, we are enabled to seek our portion and enjoyment in things above. Note well the words of Thomas Manton on this subject:

> King is a name of honour, power, and ample possession. Here we reign spiritually, as we vanquish the devil, the world, and the flesh in any measure. It is a princely thing to be above those inferior things and to trample them under our feet in a holy and heavenly pride. A heathen could say, "He is a king that fears nothing and desires nothing." He that is above the hopes and fears of the world, he that hath his heart in heaven and is above temporal trifles, the ups and downs of the world, the world beneath his affections; this man is of a kingly spirit. Christ's kingdom is not of this world, neither is a believer's. "Thou . . . hast made us unto our God kings and priests: and we shall reign on the earth" (Rev. 5:10), namely, in a *spiritual* way. It is a beastly thing to serve our lusts, but kingly to have our conversation in heaven and vanquish the world—to live up to our faith and love with a noble spirit. Hereafter we shall reign visibly and gloriously when we shall sit upon thrones with Christ.

The saints will yet judge the world, yea, and angels also (I Cor. 6:2, 3).

The Superiority of Self-Government over Secular Rule

The work that is assigned to the Christian as a king is *to govern himself*. "He that is slow to anger is better than the mighty; and he that *ruleth his spirit* than he that taketh a city" (Prov. 16:32, ital. mine). As a king the Christian is called on to mortify his own flesh, to resist the devil, to discipline his temper, to subdue his lusts, and to bring into captivity every thought to the obedience of Christ (II Cor. 10:5). That is a lifelong task. Nor can the Christian accomplish it in his own strength. It is his duty to seek enablement from above, and to draw upon the fullness of grace that is available for him in Christ. The heart is his kingdom (Prov. 4:23); and it is his responsibility to make reason and conscience, both formed by God's Word, to govern his desires so that his will is subject to God. He is required to be the master of his appetites and the regulator of his affections, to deny ungodly and worldly lusts, and to live soberly, righteously, and godly in this present world. He is to be "temperate in all things" (I Cor. 9:25). He is to subdue his impetuosity and impatience, to refuse to take revenge when others wrong him, to bridle his passions, to "overcome evil with good" (Rom. 12:21), and to have such control of himself that he "rejoice[s] with trembling" (Ps. 2:11, brackets mine). He is to learn contentment in every state or condition of life that God in His wise and good providence may be pleased to put him (Phil. 4:11).

Some earthly monarchs have not a few faithless and unruly subjects who envy and hate them, who chafe under their scepter, and who want to depose them. Nevertheless, they still maintain their thrones. In like manner, the Christian king has many rebellious lusts and traitorous dispositions that oppose and continually resist his rule, yet he must seek grace to restrain them. Instead of expecting defeat, it is his privilege to be assured, "I can do all things through Christ which strengtheneth me" (Phil. 4:13). The Apostle Paul was exercising his royal office when he declared, "all things are lawful for me, but I will not be brought under the power of any" (I Cor. 6:12). Therein he has left us an example (I Cor. 11:1). He was also conducting himself as a king when he said, "But I keep under my body, and bring it into subjection" (I Cor. 9:27). Yet, like everything else in this life, the *exercise* of our regal office is very imperfect. Not yet have we fully entered into our royal honors or acted out our royal dignity. Not yet have we received the crown, or sat down with Christ on His throne, which ceremonies of coronation are essential for the complete manifestation of our kingship. Yet the crown is laid up for us, a mansion (infinitely surpassing Buckingham Palace) is being prepared for us, and this promise is ours: "the God of peace shall bruise Satan under your feet shortly" (Rom. 16:20).

The Sacerdotal Privileges and Duties of the Believer

Following my usual custom, I have endeavored to supply the most help where the commentators and other expositors afford the least. Having sought to explain at some length the kingly office of the believer, less needs to be said upon the sacerdotal office. A priest is one who is given a place of nearness to God, who has access to Him, who holds holy intercourse with Him. It is his privilege to be admitted into the Father's presence and to be given special tokens of His favor. He has a Divine service to perform. His office is one of high honor and dignity (Heb. 5:4, 5). However, it pertains to no ecclesiastical hierarchy, but is common to *all believers*. "But ye are a chosen generation, a royal priesthood." Christians are "an holy priesthood" ordained "to offer up spiritual sacrifices, acceptable to God by Jesus Christ" (I Peter 2:5, 9). They are worshipers of the Divine majesty, and bring with them a sacrifice of praise (Heb. 13:15). "The priest's lips should keep knowledge, and they should seek the law at his mouth" (Mal. 2:7). As priests they are to be intercessors for all men, especially for kings and for all that are in authority (I Tim. 2:1, 2). But the full and perfect exercise of our priesthood lies in the future, when, rid of sin and carnal fears, we shall see God face to face and worship Him uninterruptedly.

A Fitting Doxology Based on Who Christ Is and What He Has Done

"To him be glory and dominion for ever and ever. Amen." This is an act of worship, an ascription of praise, a breathing of adoration to the Redeemer from the hearts of the redeemed. Christians vary a great deal in their capacities and attainments, and they differ in many minor views and practices. But they all unite with the apostle in this. All Christians have substantially the same views of Christ and the same love for Him. Wherever the Gospel has been savingly apprehended, it cannot but produce this effect. First there is a devout acknowledgment of what the Lord Jesus has done for us, and then a doxology rendered to Him. As we contemplate *who* it was that loved us—not a fellow mortal, but the everlasting God— we cannot but prostrate ourselves before Him in worship. As we consider *what* He did for us—shed His precious blood—our hearts are drawn out in love to Him. As we realize *how* He has bestowed such marvelous dignities upon us—made us kings and priests—we cannot but cast our crowns at His feet (Rev. 4:10). Where such sentiments truly possess the soul, Christ will be accorded the throne of our hearts. Our deepest longing will be to please Him and to live to His glory.

"To him be *glory*." This is a word that signifies (1) visible brightness or splendor, or (2) an excellence of character that places a person (or thing) in a position of good reputation, honor, and praise. The "glory of God" denotes primarily the excellence of the Divine being and the perfections of His character. The "glory of Christ" comprehends His essential Deity, the moral perfections of His humanity, and the high worth of all His offices. Secondarily, the physical manifestations of the glory of Jehovah (Exod. 3:2-6; 13:21, 22) and of His Anointed (Matt. 17:1-9) are derived from the great holiness of the triune God (Exod. 20:18, 19; 33:17-23; Judg. 13:22; I Tim. 6:16). Christ has an intrinsic glory as God the Son (John 17:5). He has an official glory as the God-man Mediator (Heb. 2:9). He has a merited glory as the reward of His work, and this He shares with His redeemed (John 17:5). In our text *glory* is ascribed to Him for each of the following reasons. Christ is here magnified both for the underived excellence of His Person that exalts Him infinitely above all creatures and for His acquired glory that will yet be displayed before an assembled universe. There is a glory that exalts Him infinitely above all creatures and for His acquired glory as the Redeemer that will yet be displayed before an assembled universe. There is a glory pertaining to Him as God incarnate, and this was proclaimed by the angels over the plains of Bethlehem (Luke 2:14). There is a glory belonging to Him in consequence of His mediatorial office and work, and that can be appropriately celebrated only by the redeemed.

"And *dominion*." This, too, belongs to Him first *by right* as the eternal God. As such Christ's dominion is underived and supreme. As such He has absolute sovereignty over all creatures, the devil himself being under His sway. Furthermore, universal dominion is also His *by merit*. God has made "that same Jesus," whom men crucified, "both

Lord and Christ" (Acts 2:36). All authority is given to Him both in heaven and in earth (Matt. 28:18). It was promised Him in the everlasting covenant as the reward of His great undertaking. The mediatorial kingdom of Christ is founded upon His sacrificial death and triumphant resurrection. These dignities of His are "for ever and ever," for "Of the increase of his government and peace there shall be no end" (Isa. 9:7; cf. Dan. 7:13, 14). By a faithful "Amen" let us set our seal to the truthfulness of God's declaration.

How blessed is this, that before any announcement is made of the awful judgments described in the Apocalypse, before a trumpet of doom is sounded, before a vial of God's wrath is poured on the earth, the saints (by John's inspired benediction) are *first* heard lauding in song the Lamb:

> Unto him that loved us, and washed us from our sins in his own blood, And hath made us kings and priests [not unto ourselves, but] unto God and his Father [for his honor]; to him be glory and dominion for ever and ever. Amen!